EMMA
A Will to Surrender

IT WAS A TRAGIC ACCIDENT, BUT MUST SHE REALLY GO TO JAIL?

EMMA
A Will to Surrender

LANCASTER COUNTY
PRISON

Becky McGurrin

ISBN-10: 1-932676-89-9
ISBN-13: 978-1-932676-89-1

Also available as E-book:
ePUB-10: 1-932676-94-5
ePUB-13: 978-1-932676-94-5
ePDF-10: 1-932676-96-1
ePDF-13: 978-1-932676-96-9

Printed in the United States of America

Cover Design and Text Layout: Naomi Yoder

All scriptures taken from the King James Version.

For special discounts on bulk purchases, please contact:
Vision Publishers Orders by phone: 877.488.0901

For Information or Comments, Please Contact:
Vision Publishers
P.O. Box 190
Harrisonburg, VA 22803
Phone: 877.488.0901
Fax: 540.437.1969
E-mail: orders@vision-publishers.com
www.vision-publishers.com
(See order form in back)

Holmes Printing Solutions
8757 County Road 77 • Fredericksburg, Ohio 44627
888.473.6870

For Jolene and Regina,
without whose vision and assistance
this story would still be hiding
in Emma's journals.

Table of Contents

Foreword

I sat in the window of the Italian bakery in old-town Lancaster munching an eggplant panino and pondering the unlikely series of events that had brought a conservative Mennonite woman from the heart of Pennsylvania to be tried for manslaughter in the courthouse across the street.

Her name was Emma Hurst, and I had been tracking down her story for the past four months—searching court records, scanning microfiched newspapers, and devouring two boxes of her personal journals and loose papers—to the point where I knew her so well, I could say that, in a way, I had become Emma.

And though I have taken the author's customary prerogative to change names, blend events, and create dialogue as the story demands, the events you are about to read are essentially those as were described by Emma herself in the pages of her journals.

CHAPTER 1

Out of the Blue

Emma struggled to open her eyes, but they were too heavy, or disconnected, or somehow very far away. It would be so much easier to surrender to the half consciousness that swirled about her head and flowed down to the tips of her fingers, barely perceptible at the furthest reaches of her awareness. But she was a Hurst, and Hursts never surrendered.

She forced her arm to move, to reach over almost instinctively to where her sister lay beside her. But Katie's spot was empty. That wasn't right.

Perhaps Emma wasn't awake after all, and this was just some freakish dream pretending to be reality. Perhaps she had merely to give in to the compulsion to sleep, or to pass out, and everything would be normal when she woke up for real.

Something shuffled beside the bed. Then someone breathed, and Emma knew that she was indeed awake, and that something was very, very wrong.

She forced her eyes to open. It was still night—the lack of sunlight through the window confirmed that—and yet she could distinctly make out the delicate scroll of white on the blue wallpaper beside her. Why was the light on in the middle of the night? And where was Katie?

"Emma," called a voice through the haze. It was Mam. She was bending over her daughter with worried eyes. Pap was right beside her. "Emma, are you all right?"

"Do I have a boyfriend?" Emma asked in reply, as if the question made any sense.

"Yes," said Mam with a catch in her voice.

"Well, who is it?"

"Don't you know?"

"No."

Emma lay still again. She was almost eighteen—of course she had a boyfriend. Frank. Yes, Frank Eby. No, it was Christ. Or was it John? It was so hard to think.

Emma forced her eyes open again and looked at her mother with anxious questions. "What's wrong?" she asked.

Mam's right hand slipped up and gripped her mouth, as if she were holding something back, as if speaking would give life to her fears.

. . . .

Emma was hungry when she woke the next morning. Sunlight flooding the room announced that the hour for breakfast had long since passed. Why hadn't Katie wakened her? She pushed back the layers of quilts that shielded her from the Pennsylvania winter and immediately regretted it. Nineteen thirty-five was a cold year.

Then she remembered her mother's anxious face framed by the pattern in the wallpaper the night before. Hadn't she passed out or something? She half remembered her mother whispering words like seizure and epilepsy to her father as she had fallen back to sleep.

Emma dressed quickly, allowing thoughts of breakfast to distract her from any further worries about the night before. It was still March—too early for fried potatoes—so breakfast was sure to be either pudding or fried mush. Either would suit; she was ravenous.

Besides, Mam wasn't a doctor. How could she tell a seizure from a nightmare—or a passing bout with a bad stomach? Then again, Mam's brother had suffered from seizures.

Thankfully, no one said much about it when Emma got to the table. Of course, everyone had already scattered to their various chores by the time she got there, so they couldn't have said much even if they had wanted to. Still, the lone plate of mush waiting for her in the middle of the table was silent testimony to the fact that something unusual had happened.

Emma was comforted by the group denial. It meant she could go on with her life as if nothing had happened. That is, until she had another spell just six weeks after the first one—again in the middle of the night. Apparently this wasn't some passing flu.

. . . .

"I'm sorry to tell you, Miss Hurst, but your mother is right," said Dr. Wenger, the man who had cared for Emma since she was a baby. "The fainting spells, as you call them, were most probably seizures. And since I can't find any reason why a girl as

healthy as you should be having seizures, we're probably looking at a case of epilepsy."

"Epilepsy? But how did I get it?"

"Sometimes people develop epilepsy after a fall or some other
brain injury, but for most people, it just comes out of the blue."

"Can you cure it?"

"No. But we can do a fairly good job of treating it with medication. I'm going to start you on a bit of phenobarbital and see
if that does the trick. I don't want to give you too much at first
because it might make you drowsy. We can always increase the
dose later if you need more."

Emma took the medication, though she was not happy with
the idea, especially since—just like the doctor had warned—it
did make her drowsy. Nor was it the cure-all she hoped it would
be, for whenever she was under an unusual amount of stress
or low on sleep, a seizure would overpower the medicine and
throw her body into violent fits.

Usually when that happened, her tongue would suck back
against her throat, causing her to hold her breath. Pap was afraid
she might choke to death.

"Emma," he said after a few of these breakthrough spells, "I
made you this here block to keep you from choking. I'm gonna
tie it to your bed and whenever you feel a spell coming on, I
want you shove it in your mouth like this . . ." He demonstrated
by placing the thin wooden block gently over his tongue and
sliding it back in his mouth.

Emma didn't know what to say, but she had a suspicion she
wasn't going to be very successful holding a stick in her mouth
when she was convulsing. Oh well, what Pap wanted, Pap got.

"I'll try," was all she said.

Frank Hurst (Emma's Pop)

And she did try. But it was as she suspected. Not only couldn't she hold onto the block once the seizures began, but she bit down upon it so tenaciously that she would often find, on coming to, that her cheeks and gums were bruised and torn from the uncontrolled battle between the block and her teeth.

But that was only a physical pain, and she could deal with it easily enough. The emotional pain—that was almost unbearable. So far, all of her seizures had been at night, and she had been very careful to keep those a secret; so she was fairly sure that no one outside the family knew she was an epileptic.

But, what if she would be seized during the daytime? What if she would go into a spell at the store, or at church, or at singing school? That would be the end of everything.

There was a way to fix that though—she could just stay home. Of course she couldn't stay home always—she did have to go to church—but even there she could sit on the back bench of the old ladies' section so she could make a quick escape through the anteroom if she felt a spell coming on.

It seemed like a good plan—if you could call a dateable young lady sitting among women three times her age good—but it was crippling to her spiritual life. While others sang *O God Our Help in Ages Past* or listened to the sermon, Emma clenched her fists and broke out in a cold sweat as her mind rehearsed a silent litany of *what if it happens now?*

And singing school? Noah and Katie would just have to go without her. She would force herself to be content singing with her family at home.

She could hear a bunch of them in the stripping shed even now, boisterously accompanying the Victrola as they sorted tobacco leaves into wrappers and fillers.

the tobacco stripping shed

Clickety clack a clunk a clunk,
The train is coming a junk a junk,
Clickety clack a mile away,
He hasn't a second of time to stay,
He sings a noisy rickety song.
A rickety rackety rockety song.

Noah's booming voice rose above the others on the final line:

> I'm on the track,
> Get out of the way,
> Go lonnnngggg.

Only when the song, and the laughter that inevitably erupted afterward, faded into relative stillness did Emma hear that her mother was singing too, as she sat on the edge of the porch watching Paul and Frank toddle on the lawn. A half-filled laundry basket sat, forgotten, by her side.

> . . . When we in the judgment stand,
> In that mighty company,
> And the Judge will question me,
> Oh, what shall my answer be?

Her mother's song was true enough, Emma supposed. It was more spiritual than the stuff that radiated out of the Victrola, at any rate. Still, if she was forced to choose only one, Emma would have to say that she found more hope in the clickety clack of the train.

CHAPTER 2

A Change of Mind

It was a delicate time for the Mennonites in Lancaster County, a time when words like hormones and hysterectomies were hinted at but never said outright. So, in the spring of 1936, when Mam went off to the hospital accompanied by silent nods and hushed whispers, Emma could guess what was going on.

She missed Mam of course, but as the oldest child in the family, she had the decided privilege of bossing the others around. Then again, she also had the responsibility of making sure all the work got done.

She sat down at the kitchen table to plan out her afternoon. Let's see, the laundry was already on the line, the menfolk all had their haircuts, and the garden was too young to need much attention. She might actually get to work on that cupboard she was planning to build in the storage room.

"What are you hatching?" asked Pap, as he walked in and saw her scanning the ceiling as if great plans were sketching themselves upon its clean white surface.

"I thought I might like to start on that cupboard."

"What are you going to do about the crooked floor?"

"That's what I was thinking about. I could just cut the footer with the same slant as the floor, and you'd never know the difference from the top."

"You can't go making a crooked cupboard just so it fits in a crooked room! You'd have to leave it there forever."

"Well, I wasn't planning on moving it."

"If you say so, Emma, but it's the strangest way I ever heard of building a cupboard, and that's a fact."

They looked up together as they heard the frantic tramp of heavy feet and shouts rushing from the other side of the house.

the home place (dawdi house on the left)

"Frank! Frank! Come!" Pap's father shouted as he burst into the room. His aged face was flushed with confusion and distress.

"Frank! Hurry! Something is wrong with Mummi! Please, come right away!"

Emma followed the men as they raced through the parlor to the far end of the building where her grandparents lived in their own little Dawdi house.

Emma stopped in horror when she saw her grandmother, crouched forward in her chair, gasping for breath. The skin on her cheeks was pale as bread dough, and her eyes stared at Emma like a shied horse.

Pap knelt on the floor beside the chair and grabbed Mummi's sweaty hand. "What is it, Mummi? What's wrong?"

Mummi grabbed Pap's shirt and begged him with her wide, frantic eyes. "I can't . . . breathe . . . here." She gripped her chest.

Frank looked at his father. "Is she choking?"

"No, we finished supper a half hour ago and she was fine. Laughing and smiling like she always does. And then she just grabbed her dress like you see there and started to breathe like that. What's wrong?"

"I don't know. She doesn't have a cold or anything?"

"No. She was fine."

Mummi sucked in a large breath and slumped back in the chair, her mare's eyes rolling up behind their lids and freezing there. She was gone.

Emma had no time to cry. There was the funeral to arrange, clothes to prepare, and several week's work of spring cleaning to catch up on before people came for visitation—and no mother to help her with any of it.

By the time Mam got home from the hospital, Mummi had been buried, Grandfather was alone, and the Dawdi house was quiet and still. Pap fixed Mam a bed in the living room where she could be out among the family as she regained her strength, but her homecoming only added to Emma's burdens.

"Dear," she would ask as Emma passed through the room with a basket of laundry, "would you mind fixing those curtains over there? Paul mussed them up when he was looking out for Pap and Noah . . . and, could you tell the girls to quiet down a bit up there? The noise wears on me, you know . . . and, do you suppose you could sit in here with me a spell? I wouldn't mind a bit of company."

And on and on it went with Emma stopping in the middle of every task, it seemed, to do something or redo something to make Mam more comfortable.

The extra stress, at a time when she should have been openly grieving for her grandmother, began to show. Each additional worry, each additional responsibility, each night with not enough sleep brought on new seizures, each spell adding to the exhaustion and stress that were already more than she could handle. No medication could keep seizures from breaking through an onslaught like this.

One Sunday afternoon, the thing that she had feared most happened—she had a seizure in front of visitors. They were folks from the Martindale church who had come to visit Mam where she lay in the living room. Emma hadn't gotten much sleep the night before, and this being a Sunday, and that a day of rest, she said a respectable hello and slipped off to the adjoining parlor to sneak in a little quiet time by herself.

The parlor was the perfect place to get away, with its soft furniture blanketed in warm sunlight and a door that Emma could shut to the world.

She eased herself onto the sofa. Ahh. She slipped off her shoes, pulled up her feet, and stretched out on the cushions. There, that was even nicer.

the parlor in the home place

She leaned back her head just a bit and listened to the bees contentedly humming around the flowers beyond the open window. Their sound was soft and rhythmic, almost musical, like a lullaby.

Emma woke with a start. A seizure was building in her brain. She could feel it in her throat and her stomach, almost like a smell, but in the wrong place.

Oh no. The visitors! They were right beyond the paper-thin door. She could hear their Sunday voices from where she sat, could almost make out their very words. They would be able to hear her choking and thrashing just as easily. What could she do?

The seizure was almost upon her; she had only seconds.

She frantically looked around for something to shove in her mouth, something to muffle the noises. What? There was nothing; not a spoon, not a doorstop . . . the blanket! She could use the blanket resting on the arm of the sofa. With her last conscious effort she grabbed the blanket and thrust it deep into her throat. Then she blacked out.

Emma came to on the kitchen floor. The kitchen? How had she gotten here? The kitchen was fully across the building on the other side of the house. The only way she could have gotten here was through the living room.

the living room through which Emma walked while having a seizure

Then she saw them—the visitors. They were gathered around her, gaping down at the spectacle she was making of herself.

"Are you okay, Emma?" It was Pap, leaning close and whispering in her ear. "It seems you had a little spell. You walked all the way in here from the parlor with that blanket in your mouth. I could tell you were seizing the whole time, but I don't reckon they knew what was going on. Here, let me help you to your room."

With that, Pap helped Emma to her feet, put his arm around her, and escorted her upstairs, being careful the whole time to keep his body, like a shield, between his daughter and those who would know her secret shame.

Emma longed to run into her mother's arms and sit there like she had when she was Frank's age, to be held and petted and have all the tears wiped away. But Emma was not a baby anymore. Neither was Mam able to offer much comfort.

Her surgical wounds had healed well enough, but the rest of her—the part that had been Mam since Emma was a little girl—had dimmed and transformed until she was barely recognizable as the same woman.

At first she was just moody—crying for no apparent reason, or laughing when nothing was funny. Then she started to do inexplicable things like lying down on the floor after she was dressed to go outside, or acting like she was the guest at her own dinner table. And by the time the maple leaves had displayed the first premature hints of red, Mam had come to believe that someone was out to get her.

"Please, Mam, try to eat something," encouraged Emma, as she set a sandwich and a glass of tea on the table. It was well past mid-day, and Emma was sure her mother hadn't eaten a bite since the apple she had scrubbed and peeled for herself that morning.

"I'm not hungry."

"You have to eat something to keep up your strength."

"Did your father make it?"

"I did."

"Did he touch the meat?"

"No, I fixed all the ingredients myself, and I washed my hands before I began. Really, Mam, I'm sure it's good healthy food. Please eat it."

Mam sneered at the sandwich. Then she turned her head ever so slightly and peeked out from half-closed eyes to the parlor.

No one was there. She nibbled a corner of the crust and left the glass untouched.

Emma heard Pap's whistle bouncing in from the back screen door; he must have gotten that silo ladder fixed. He did hate a rickety ladder.

Mam heard the whistle too, and before Pap got fully into the room or could say as much as a hello ladies, Mam had fled from the room and was bolting up the stairs.

Emma looked at her father with an expression of mixed embarrassment, sympathy, and apology.

"Heard me coming, did she?"

"Mm-hm."

"Is that her lunch?"

"What's left of it. She wasn't hungry."

"The woman's gonna kill herself, not eating like that."

"She's convinced we're the ones trying to kill her."

"Bah, it's just me. Seems to think I'm her sworn enemy. I have to wrap her nightgown around my arm when she sleeps or she'll up and run away in the middle of the night."

"It's her mind, you know. Ever since that surgery."

"I know." Pap pursed his lips and looked at his boots.

"Do you think we should tell the doctor? He might have some ideas."

"I already did. He said we might want to hire a nurse. Maybe she'll trust a stranger."

Emma's eyes moistened. Poor Pap. He would do anything for Mam.

But none of his efforts got through to Mam's ailing mind—the more he tried to help her, serve her, coddle her, and protect her from harm, the more she was convinced that he wanted her dead, and she despised him for all his efforts.

It about broke Emma's heart.

One evening in mid October, Noah and Katie persuaded Emma to come out with them to a singing. Things with Mam had gotten so bad, she would almost rather have a seizure in front of every young person in the Weaverland Conference than spend one more evening watching her father's heart get crushed by his wife's broken mind.

The lights were still on in the kitchen when they got home close to midnight, and Alta's tiny face was peeking at them out the back window. She should have been in bed hours ago.

They entered the kitchen to find Pap standing there waiting for them. All the children were up, gathered around the table with a very-late-night snack.

"What's up?" Noah asked.

"Mam's not feeling well," Pap said over the catch in his voice. "I think she's dying."

"What!"

"She wants to see all of you together. I want you little ones to go right up to the bed with nice big smiles on your faces and you older ones can gather in behind. Squeeze in close so she can see all of you."

One by one the children filed into their parents' room and gathered, like Ephraim and Manasseh, around their mother's bed—Emma, Katie, and Noah; Lydia and Mary; Esther and Alta, with Paul and Frank in their oldest sisters' arms.

Mam looked at each of them in turn. Gone was the suspicion, the paranoia, the reclusiveness. In their place was their calm and lucid mother.

"Children, I'm not well. Doctor Wenger says I may have a bad heart. I won't be with you much longer, and I want to tell you some important things."

She prayed for each child by name, for their lives, their futures, and for all their precious little souls.

"I want you all to be good children. Obey your father and grow up to be good, strong, holy men and women. And when you get to heaven, I will be waiting for you."

Then she laid her head back on the pillow and closed her eyes. Her skin cooled to the touch and her breathing softened. The children quietly left the room, some with tears in their eyes, others in shock. Their mother had returned to her right mind just long enough to tell them she was leaving them.

To everyone's surprise, Mam was warm and stronger in the morning. But it was only a cruel trick, for even as her body rallied, her sweet spirit slipped back into the tangled threads of a deranged mind.

And even that was only temporary. Mam developed a case of pneumonia that sparred with her throughout the following winter. When her lungs were swollen with fluid, her mind was sweet and lucid. And when her lungs were clear, her mind was not. Strong then weak. Deranged then sane. What kind of cruel torture was this?

Emma reeled with each new blow, ashamed to admit, even to herself, that she wished at times that Mam would just die and let all of them live in peace. Dare she tell God how angry she was? How bitterly outraged and hopeless?

But God knew, as He had known all along, and on April 17, when the grass was green and the goldfinches were flaunting their brightest yellows, Mam mercifully slipped off into that land where all minds are clear and love is predictable and undying.

Frank Hurst (Pop) with his children in 1937

The Hurst family breathed a collective sigh of relief. Then they grieved.

Emma reeled with conflicting surges of emotion. She was the oldest woman now in a family of ten, and there was no Mam to help her think, or plan, or make sense out of life. There was no one to sit on the porch swing with her and talk about which boy might ask her to go with him to the next singing. Not that it mattered anymore. The epilepsy had wiped out any prospects in that direction.

She ran out the back door, past the silo, to the farthest corner of the orchard where there was nothing but trees, and echoes, and the big empty sky. She heaved one great audible groan of pure anguish and let the tears fall. How she missed Mam—the real Mam. And Mummi. And life as it used to be.

She watched as the tears ran off her cheeks to spread out in dark growing circles on the cape of her black mourning dress.

Life was turning out to be nothing more than one dark, growing disappointment after another. One big empty nothing.

CHAPTER 3

A Case of Two Esthers

Emma finished hemming the dress. It was black like all the others. The Hursts were in mourning now, and the girls each needed enough black dresses to last a full year. Emma liked the sewing. But six girls meant a lot of dresses.

She set the dress on the back of the chair and headed into the kitchen. It was high time she got supper on.

Emma peeled the last potato with a sigh. It was more fit for planting than for eating really, eyes sprouting hopefully in every direction. The new potatoes wouldn't be ready for at least a month yet.

"Say, there, Emma," called Pop as the door slammed behind him. "What's for supper?"

"Potato soup, same as last night."

"Same soup or same recipe?" His eyes twinkled with his little joke. "I was wondering what you thought about the sweet corn this year. Mam always liked six rows, but as you'll be doing most of the cooking I thought you might have some other number in mind."

Pap had been asking her all sorts of questions like this since Mam had passed away. "What do you think of this here New Deal the President worked up, Emma? Do you suppose it'll rain this afternoon, Emma? Say, Emma, how is Alta coming along on her reading?"

Why, he had even been confiding more personal things to her: how stressful life was, how difficult the future looked, how much he missed Mam.

Emma liked the new closeness and the confidence he placed in her. Being the woman in the home wasn't turning out to be so bad after all.

Then one day toward the end of the year, before the mound over Mam's grave had settled into a decent flatness, Pap brought home Esther. Not his daughter, Esther, but a pretty woman, barely thirteen years older than Emma—and apparently much wiser.

Pap stopped confiding in Emma as suddenly as he had started. No more, Say, Emma, what do you think about this? Or, What do you reckon that? Emma felt orphaned all over again. Of course she didn't let Pap know how she felt.

Katie wasn't as discrete, and she let Pap know her feelings in plain terms. After all, Mam wasn't gone but half a year and here comes this woman—this Esther—marching into the kitchen in her light print dresses and sitting in Mam's chair like she belonged there. She even had the nerve to pick up Frank and cuddle him like he was her own. Well, he wasn't, and she'd better not forget it!

Katie

Stomp! went Katie's heel one day as she pounded her shoe into Pap's unsuspecting foot. Apparently he thought the game of footsie he had been enjoying with his lady friend had gone unnoticed by the children gathered around the table. But Katie saw the whole thing and was disgusted by his heartless expression of affection.

"Put away your black dresses," he told the girls the next day, "and pull out your pretty prints."

"But, Pap," said Emma in astonishment, "what about the mourning?"

"The mourning in this house is officially over. Esther and I will be getting married in January, and it wouldn't look right for you girls to wear black during an engagement."

Emma swallowed hard. "Isn't January a little soon? I mean, with Mam's death being just in the spring and all."

"If your tractor dies, you don't wait a year to get another one. And you children have been without a mother long enough."

Emma didn't dare say what she really thought, that Mam wasn't a tractor, and the whole thing was shockingly soon. But she obeyed, neatly packing away the girls' dark dresses and pulling their lighter prints to the front of the closet.

Pap was right in a way, the children did need a mother. But hadn't she been that mother for the past six months? What was wrong with the way she cared for them?

She knew Pap's real reason for wanting Esther. He had been without a companion for as long as they had been without a mother and he was lonely. Poor man.

After the blush of Pap's announcement had faded to a dull pink, the Hursts were left with one question they could not brush aside: What should they call the new member of the family? They couldn't call her Esther because they already had an Esther in the house. Stepmother sounded inhospitably stiff. They wouldn't call her Mam; that name was sacred. What about Mom? And they could switch Pap's name to Pop at the same time so they would be a matched set. Yes, that sounded nice, Pop and Mom.

It didn't take Esther, er, Mom, long to find her place in the Hurst home, especially after Katie stopped thinking of her as Mam's replacement. She was thoughtful and hardworking, and she didn't seem to mind sitting right down beside the children and sharing in their world.

"Here," Mom said to Lydia as she gently reached over the girl's shoulder and guided her hand in the proper way to hold her crochet hook. "Hold the needle in your hand like this and place your stitches with your wrist. It'll save your hand from tiring out."

Lydia looked up and beamed. She had always wanted to learn to crochet.

"How does this look?" asked Mary, holding out her doily for inspection.

"Oh, that's lovely! Your stitches are small and even."

"I'm making this one for Katie's birthday, but she doesn't know about it."

"My lips are sealed."

Pop and Noah liked having Mom around too. She could not only cook and clean circles around the girls, but she also helped the men pull in the tobacco and strip it when they needed an extra hired man.

Mom did so much work, in fact, that Emma found herself out of a job. Not that she wasn't welcome to help, she just wasn't needed any more.

"Have you considered working down at the garment factory?" Mom asked Emma one long and dreary afternoon. "Some of the girls are making 75¢ a day, I hear, and your sewing is beautiful."

"I guess I never thought of working out. I mean, there was always so much to do around here."

"Well, I was talking with your father about it, and he said that, as you are almost twenty-one, you could keep the money you earn and start saving up for . . . well, for the future. Check into it."

"I think I will."

For all Mom's hard work and good advice though, there was one thing she just couldn't seem to do well, one thing for which she would have traded a myriad perfect stitches and well-dried tobacco leaves. No matter how carefully she watched her diet, nor how early she got to bed, Mom could not seem to bear healthy children.

It started with Lizzie. She was the tiniest baby Emma had ever seen. But she was born many weeks too soon, and before she could focus enough to gaze into her mother's loving eyes, she quietly slipped away.

Emma tenderly lifted her sister and held the lifeless body to her breast. There was no warmth, no soft butterfly breaths. The body was empty.

She carried Lizzie over to the washstand and gave the baby her farewell bath—Mom was too weak. Then she dressed her in the little gown that had been prepared for a living child and laid her body in the undersized coffin Pop had fetched from the undertaker.

They buried Lizzie's body in the church graveyard.

Ivan arrived a year and a half later. He was bigger than Lizzie, but something was wrong. He vomited so continuously that he hardly gained any weight. It was clear the boy would not thrive.

Well-wishers bombarded Mom with all manner of miracle remedies and unlikely cures, but Ivan responded to none of them. Mom steeled her heart for another disappointment.

David came another year and a half later, and he looked like the hoped-for child. He was strong, fully developed, and he had a zeal for life. While Ivan continued to vomit and languish, David bounded along like a young collie.

Then David, too, started to vomit. And his eyesight failed. And he whimpered.

Pop made continual visits to Dr. Wenger. First for Ivan, then for David, and then again for Mom. She was expecting again.

It was another boy. They named him John. The name means God is gracious. Surely this would be the child of grace, the one who would run and climb like little boys were meant to do.

But it was not to be. When John was a comfortable nine days old, he took one last peaceful breath, closed his eyes, and left his parents behind.

Mom looked to Ivan and David to comfort her aching heart, but they continued to vomit relentlessly.

"I'm sorry, Mr. Hurst," the doctor told Pop when he took David in for one more desperate visit. "I'm afraid your boy has a brain tumor."

"Is there anything . . . ?"

The doctor shook his head.

Pop and Mom buried David beside Lizzie and John.

The world took no notice of the three little graves in the Martindale Church cemetery. It had fresh graves of its own. Rather, call them trenches, or pits, or gas chambers. For, farther away than Emma could imagine, across the stormy Atlantic to the farmland and cities of Europe, thousands of children were dying hideous, premature deaths. Adolf Hitler had come to power.

Emma knew about the war, of course, but it was nothing that affected her or her people. They were Mennonites, peace people, farmers. They didn't fight in anyone's wars—especially not wars in Europe. Oh, she prayed for peace, but it was hard to wrap one's heart around the grief of foreigners. They were so far away, speaking a language she only half understood.

Now Mom's grief—that was different. She had buried three babies in as many years, and her only remaining child, with his sallow cheeks and tiny stature, was not expected to do well. That was the kind of grief Emma could feel. And whether from this

shared grief, or from empathy, or from a deep womanly understanding, Emma grew to love her stepmother deeply.

"How can you just accept all this dying?" she asked one afternoon when she caught Mom alone during Ivan's nap time.

"What do you mean?"

"All the dying—Lizzie, John, David. And Ivan, sick as he is.
You act as if you are the happiest woman in the world, and I
know you would have given your life for those babies."

"I am happy. Don't get me wrong, I would do anything to
bring them back. But we can't pick and choose which trials God
will send our way."

"You think He wanted them to die?"

"I don't mean it that way, Emma. It's like Jacob, wrestling with
God. I don't suppose he wanted to fight with God either. But he
had no choice. Jacob's problem was he didn't recognize who he
was fighting against."

"Sure, but Jacob only wrestled one night before he found out
that it was God who was his opponent. And then God blessed
him."

"God will bless us, too, if we recognize Him as the controller
of our lives and yield to that control. It's about contentment,
Emma. In whatsoever state we find ourselves, there we must be
content. So, I am content with the one tiny boy in my arms and
the three that await me on the other side."

Emma had never thought about God this way before—never
imagined that hard times might actually be a way to come to
know God better.

Is that what He wanted from her: that she would try to see
Him in her circumstances and be content with the way things

were? No, it was more than that. He wanted her to grab hold of Him and wrestle like Jacob until she knew who He really was.

It would all make a great devotional topic, but really, how does one wrap their arms around an infinite God? Well, at the least, she could start with paying more attention at church instead of worrying about herself all the time. That would be good advice anytime. And maybe she should consider singing more hymns and less train songs. And she could wear plainer, more conservative dresses. Yes, and she could even trade in her jacket for a shawl. All the older ladies wore shawls and they were definitely serious about living for God.

Of course, the girls at the garment factory would give her a regular dressing down if she showed up to work in a shawl. So what? God had taken hold of Emma Hurst and she was going to wrestle back.

CHAPTER 4

Grandpa's Old Bookshelf

World War II burst upon the Mennonites in 1941 when government men came to Martindale and arrested Emma's non-resistant neighbors as they were threshing in their fields. It exploded on the Hursts when Noah received a letter from those same men. He opened it on the porch where several of the family were working up dropped apples for applesauce.

Noah read the letter without saying a word. Then he folded it back up and creased the edges.

"What's it say?" asked Pop, apparently the only one who had enough courage to ask.

Noah slowly lifted his head and looked at his father. "It says I'm supposed to report for the draft."

"Bah, you couldn't kill anybody. They ought to know that."

Emma put her hand on Pop's arm and shook her head. Tears had welled up in Noah's eyes.

"Let me see that."

Noah handed him the letter. Pop read it, then handed it back.

"Maybe they'll let you work on the forest projects like they're letting some of the men do. If they know you're a Mennonite, they surely wouldn't ask you to fight. I hear some of our guys are even jumping out of airplanes to fight fires in the Rocky Mountains."

"Yeah, can you see me jumping out of an airplane?"

Paul's eyes grew wide. "Would they give you a parachute?"

Noah smacked his little brother on the shoulder. "Yeah, snip. They'd give me a parachute. But if I went for that job, I'd have to pack you in my suitcase so I could use you to test the thing first."

Paul's eyes grew wider still. "Not me. I'm too young to fly!"

That brought the smile back to Noah's face. He looked back at his father. "I don't know, Pop. Things didn't go so well for Mennonites in the last war."

As it turned out, Noah needn't have worried. The draft board seemed to think he was more valuable on the farm than behind a gun, so they gave him a farm deferment and let him go home.

Emma was glad she was not a man. She didn't know what she would do if someone asked her to fight. It was hard enough to watch the men you love go off to war without having to go yourself.

Take Noah's girlfriend, Mabel Zimmerman. What would she have done if Noah had been sent away? Probably she'd have lain awake every night with visions of Noah falling out of airplanes or getting roughed up by the patriotic fellows in camp.

Or Katie with her boyfriend, John Horning. They were engaged to be married in January. Would they push up the wedding if he got called, in hopes that they would have pity and let him stay home with his new bride?

Not that Emma had anything like that to worry about. She hadn't dated since the epilepsy began. Oh, she still longed for a family of her own, but men had stopped calling on her. What man wants a wife who thrashes around the bed at night?

She headed into the storage room to put away the extra dish-pans they hadn't needed for the apples. As she opened the door of the cupboard, she noticed the crooked footer she had cut so carefully to make the thing stand level on the slanted floor. She smiled to herself. Her plan had worked after all. Not that Pop had ever congratulated her about it or even admitted that her idea had worked. She couldn't help laughing at the thought. Stubborn old man—but she wouldn't have him any other way!

the cabinet that Emma built to fit the slanted floor

Time for a little rest. Not a long one, just fifteen minutes or so to sit and think.

She went to the parlor and leaned her head back against the chair. Ah, that felt so good on her neck. She lazily stared at Grandpa's old bookshelf across the room. One title caught her eye, *The Christian's Secret of a Happy Life*. She had never noticed that one before.

She looked at the spine. It was by Hannah Whitall Smith. Never heard of her. But the book was old and the threads on the corners of the cover frayed, as if from a frequent fond embrace. This must have been one of her grandfather's favorites.

She flipped to the title page. Eighteen seventy-five. The book was almost sixty-five years old. Then again, age does not automatically imply obsolescence. Perhaps Mrs. Smith had something interesting to say.

Emma slipped up to the sewing room Pop had fixed up for her when Grandpa had moved out of the Dawdi house a few years before. The applesauce could wait.

Emma's pair of rooms in the Dawdi house

She checked the coals in the small egg stove that heated the little room. They glowed warm and red. She settled herself in her chair and began to read.

. . . We cannot hope to reach this maturity in any other way than by yielding ourselves completely and willingly to His mighty working. . . . Our part is the trusting. His part is to accomplish the results.

This sounded just like what Mom had said about wrestling with God. He oversees the details of our lives, and we must trust that He knows what is best. But what is this about the will?

. . . [A lady] had learned the secret of the will, and knowing that she had chosen the will of God for her portion, she didn't pay the slightest attention to her emotions. She persisted in confronting every thought concerning [her] trial with the words, "Thy will be done! Thy will be done!" That His will should be done was her delight! The result was that in an incredibly short space of time every thought was brought into captivity, and she began to find even her emotions rejoicing in the will of God.

Could a person really be happy letting God do whatever He wanted in their life? Mom seemed to be. But what about Emma herself? She wasn't sure if she was willing to let God do anything. Oh, she had stopped whining about the epilepsy, but she was pretty sure she wouldn't want God to send her into a fit right in the middle of a church service. That would be asking a lot.

But what if God did want her to trust Him on that level? After all, if He really was good, and if He really was in control of the universe, then everything He allowed to happen to her would somehow be for the good. Wouldn't it?

And all she would have to do to be happy with His choices was to be willing to accept them; right?

Then again, this was the God who had allowed Mom to lose three babies.

Ach, Emma! You have no faith!

Perhaps she could test the idea by going off the phenobarbital for a while to see what God did with her seizures. After all, a person with real faith could certainly trust Him to handle her medical decisions. Couldn't she? She put that night's medicine back into the pill box. She was going to live by faith.

. . . .

Emma was overcome by seizures that first night—and for many nights after. And they were hard, vicious seizures. Esther and Mary, in the room beside hers, told her they were sure she would die from the violence of her thrashing. She almost wished she could.

She briefly thought about going back on the medicine. But what if the spells were sent by God to test her resolve? No, she had to prove her faith.

But, as the days and weeks went by with no decrease in attacks, Emma reconsidered. If God had been testing her, she would surely have proved herself by now. It was more likely that she had shocked her system by removing the drugs too suddenly. Perhaps she should go on the medicine again, just for a short while, then come off again more slowly. Yes, that was what she would do.

She resumed her nightly dose of phenobarbital until the spells went away again. Then she slowly weaned herself off the medicine, shaving just a sliver from each pill before she took it. Then more slivers, and more until, after many weeks, her body was totally free from all medicine.

This time she had only an occasional seizure—just enough to remind her of who was in control—what a precious gift! Thy will be done, Lord! Thy will be done!

Then she thought about all the things she had been doing to win God's favor—the dark dresses, the shawl, acting like an old

woman—and she realized they were nothing like the real surrender she was experiencing in letting God control her health.

She went to her closet and pulled out the summer-blue dimity
dress hidden in the back. When she put it on and looked at herself in the mirror, she couldn't help but smile. If she was going to
have seizures for God, she was going to look cheerful while she
did so. Thy will be done, Lord! Thy will be done!

She no longer felt heartsick that men had stopped asking to
escort her to singings. Nor did it sting when Lydia announced
her engagement to marry Ivan Hoover that fall.

Though she had to admit that it did feel odd to have Mary
be the next oldest sibling in the house. Little Mary, the next in
line. Did that make Emma the old maid? The thought made her
chuckle. Emma Hurst, an old maid. Who could have imagined
such a thing?

Hurst Girls 1934 L-R: Alta, Lydia, Emma, Mary, Esther

Then again, while she had been hanging around wrestling
with God and His will, her entire family had aged. Esther was,
what, seventeen? And Alta had just turned fourteen. Her baby
sister, fourteen!

The boys were sneaking up on her, too. Paul was twelve already and Frank was ten and Ivan—puny little Ivan—was fast catching up at four. Is this how it is for old people watching their loved ones age before their eyes? No matter.

Mom loved to tease Emma about her old-maid status. "Well, my dear," she would say with a grin and a wink, "I do believe you can do just about anything you set your mind to, everything, that is, except get a man."

Emma grinned back. She didn't mind the teasing. Not much anyway. Besides, each time one of her siblings got married she gained a sibling of sorts.

Like Katie's John. He was a rare find. Proper as all-git-out on the outside, but with a touch of Hurst just below the surface. He was perfect for Katie, and everyone else loved him too. The boys especially liked to try to catch him with some little joke or prank when they were sorting tobacco leaves.

"Say, John," asked Paul with a poorly-disguised grin in his voice, "What do you think of this leaf here? Is it a wrapper or a filler?"

John looked over the leaf in question and quickly proclaimed it a filler. The leaf was border-line, as Paul had known before he asked John about it, so Paul quietly tucked it back in his own pile.

When he came upon the same leaf again, quite a while later, he took it to John again and asked. "Say John, what about this one? Would you call it a wrapper or a filler?"

John looked the leaf over closely. Then he grinned. "Hey! You had that here before! And it's still a filler."

Emma liked John, too, though he did need some training on how to tell a joke. That was okay though. A few more years with Katie and he'd be as good as a Hurst.

CHAPTER 5

Duke Street

Downtown Lancaster was a symphony for the senses: fabulous architecture, aromatic, Old-world bakeries, flashing traffic signals, and all manner of horns and bells. Trolley cars owned the central third of the busiest streets. Parked cars and milling people claimed the rest. It was the sort of place that would delight any adventurer. For the motorist, it was a nightmare.

Emma made a right onto Duke Street. She was taking her neighbors to visit their father in the Lancaster hospital. It was 7 p.m., and the shadows were already long on the pavement.

"I sure do appreciate you driving us like this, Emma," said Anna Mae Sensenig, the graceful young lady in the passenger's seat.

"Oh, it's no trouble. I like driving."

"Papa will be so glad to see us. You remember about the package we want to drop off?"

"Your friend lives on Lemon Street, right?"

"Mm-hm."

"I think that's right past the hospital. We'll go there first, then head up to see your father after we have dropped it off."

Emma didn't mind driving her neighbors. None of them had licenses and she did. Besides, she was twenty-nine, had plenty of time on her hands, and doing favors gave her a sense of purpose. But these city streets were nothing like her quiet country roads; they fired distractions from so many angles, and she had to work hard to concentrate. Not to mention, she was driving Mr. Sensenig's car, and it didn't handle quite like Pop's.

Let's see, Lemon Street should be up beyond that row of houses, right about where that streetcar is. No, maybe it was a bit further on. Now what did that street sign say? Emma squinted her eyes in an attempt to make out the letters. Eyeglasses were nice, but they didn't give one telescopic vision. Fredrick. It was Fredrick Street; where was Lemon?

She was almost even with the streetcar now, and it seemed to be slowing down. That didn't make any sense; the traffic light was still green. Green was the same for streetcars as it was for automobiles—wasn't it?

Emma slowed a bit as she pulled along the right side of the trolley. It was a long one, and hard to see around. Had it come to a complete stop? The car ahead of her was still moving. Maybe trolleys always stopped when they came to an intersection— to look out for new passengers, or for cars moving along the side streets.

There was a car parked along the curb to her right but she had plenty of room to slip between it and the trolley. She could see the heads of a few people standing on the curb beyond the parked car, but no one was in the streets so, she kept going.

"Wait!"

"Stop!"

"Emma!"

Several people screamed at once.

There was a slight jolt and a sickening bump as Emma's right front wheel went up and over something tiny and delicate and grindingly real.

Emma slammed on the brakes, but it was too late. Then she looked in her rearview mirror, dreading to see what she knew must lie behind her. Oh, God, no! No. It was a child. A tiny, motionless child. She lay there in the street like a broken china doll. Emma shuddered; this couldn't be real. Oh please, God, let her be alive!

She watched through glazed eyes as a man scooped up the child and cradled her in his arms as he ran to the hospital, now visible across the street, her tiny feet dangling like over-ripe apples bobbing in the wind.

Emma's thoughts were swallowed by the raw emotion that spun and swirled through her mind—a giant, sucking whirlpool.

"We will need the owner's card for the car," she said in slow, suffocating breaths, though she was neither conscious of what she said, nor even that she had spoken at all.

"Papa keeps it in his wallet. He's got it with him."

"Run and get it," Emma said with one final effort. Then she folded her arms on the steering wheel, buried her face deep in their silent shadows, and struggled to form a single rational thought.

. . . .

Emma roused from her stupor several lifetimes later, though in truth, she had appeared to be conscious the entire time. She was at the police station surrounded by hazy faces and dozens of incomprehensible questions.

"Yes, I have been driving an automobile for thirteen years. . . . No, it was the first time I have ever driven on a city one-way street—no, on this one-way street. . . . No, I did not know I could not pass a trolley car while it was loading or unloading passengers. . . . No, I didn't know the car had hit someone until Anna Mae screamed and I felt a bump . . ." and on and on, seemingly through the night.

"Emma." It was Pop. How had he gotten here? And Katie's John.

"Oh, Pop, I hit a little girl."

"I know."

"She just lay there on the street. And when the man picked her up, she hung in his arms like a doll baby. Oh, Pop. I hurt her bad."

"Listen, Emma." Were those tears in Pop's eyes? "She didn't make it. I mean, the little girl. She died pretty soon after she got to the hospital. I don't imagine she suffered much."

Emma closed her eyes and tried to hang on.

"They need to keep you here a while longer, till they figure out what went wrong exactly. I mean what her injuries were. Then they'll know what charges they might need to file against you."

"Murder."

"No, I don't think it will be that. You didn't mean any harm."

"What was her name?"

"The little girl? Crill something, I think they said. Sandra Crill."

"And Mrs. Crill?"

"I imagine folks are taking good care of her."

Emma's head dropped forward on her chest. Sandra. It was such a pretty name. And she was such a little thing.

The coroner's report came in several hours later. Sandra Crill, four years old, had died of a fractured skull. Emma was charged with involuntary manslaughter and released on $500 bail. Pop and John took her home.

The headlines in the Lancaster Intelligencer Journal the next morning, Wednesday, September 11, 1946, read, "Car Kills Girl Boarding Trolley." Emma slipped off to the outhouse, where she could shut out the headlines, and wailed like the roaring, empty wind. But it brought no relief. When at last she opened the door to confront the world, she found that it was as empty and lifeless as her bleeding heart.

CHAPTER 6

Case Number 66

Emma sat in the chair beside Pop in Attorney W. Hansel Brown's office. She didn't really need an attorney but the judge had insisted.

"You can either plead guilty," the lawyer explained across the desk, "and take whatever penalty the judge deems fair—including possibly having to pay damages to the Crill family for the loss of their child—or you could plead not-guilty, which would leave open the possibility that you could get off without serving time in jail."

"Not guilty! That would be a lie!"

"A plea of not guilty in a court of law is not quite the same as saying you are not in some way responsible. It's more like saying that things aren't as cut-and-dried as they seem, and the judgment of your case should take into account such things as your inexperience in the city, the time of day, things like that."

"Does her mother think I'm not guilty? Or her father? Surely her grandmother doesn't." Vivid memories of Sandra's grandmother hissing in Emma's face at the girl's viewing still haunted her. "You're not fit to be on the road!"

No, she would plead the truth and take the punishment she deserved.

"The Crill family is asking for ten thousand dollars in damages, in addition to a hearing. If you plead guilty, you will be agreeing to pay that sum."

"I have five thousand already in the bank."

"They want ten thousand."

Emma looked at Pop. He leaned over and whispered softly. "You just go ahead and do what you have to do and we'll get the rest of the money somehow."

She looked back at Attorney Brown. "I will get the rest of the money. I wish to plead guilty."

"You will also need a few hundred dollars for court fees."

"She'll get that too," added Pop.

"All right. Your indictment, that is, the day you formally enter your plea, will probably be in November or December, depending on how full the court docket is. You will have until then to change your mind."

"I don't expect it'll change any between now and then."

Whether Emma's contrite generosity softened their hearts, or whether they had just needed some time to adjust to the magnitude of their loss, the Crills agreed within a few days to accept a settlement of only forty-five hundred dollars if Emma would still agree to a hearing before a judge.

. . . .

Duke Street was all decked out for its Christmas celebrations when Emma returned for her indictment on December 9. Bristly pines proudly displayed their delicate, glass ornaments in the bay windows of statelier homes; storefront windows twinkled with colored lights; and signs offering free gift wrapping enticed holiday shoppers to come in and have a look around. The trolley clanged its way toward Fredrick Street as if unaware that one less child would be opening gifts that year.

Emma looked up at the Lancaster County Courthouse whose massive stone pillars and Romanesque arches seemed to have been designed with one purpose—to make people feel small. Inside was not as bad, unless one brought their guilt in with them, in which case their insignificance was more than just a perception. Emma felt hollow just opening the door.

Pop put his arm on her shoulder. "You're doing the right thing, Emma."

She gave him a little half smile and subconsciously fingered the bow at the end of her covering strings.

They were both surprised at how little time it took for Emma to enter her plea. The judge asked a few questions to make sure she understood what it meant to plead guilty, then several witnesses signed the formal indictment—Officer Baltasser, who had found her in her car the day of the accident; Dr. Stahr, the coroner; and a few others.

She was listed in the official records as Docket number 66—as if she were a case, rather than a person. Perhaps she was. There certainly wasn't much personhood in having your name coupled with a charge—involuntary manslaughter. There was less in having it labeled with a plea—guilty. Number 66, Emma B. Hurst, guilty of involuntary manslaughter.

Things were more complicated on January 10, the date of her actual hearing. Two judges, Oliver S. Schaeffer and Joseph B. Wissler, sat on the bench facing the crowd that packed the room.

Attorney Brown was there, of course, sitting beside Emma at the oversized wooden table, and Officer Baltasser, and the coroner, and lawyers for the Crills, and recorders, and reporters, and, well, more people than were needed, surely!

Emma fingered her covering strings again and looked at the judges as someone made introductory remarks about the case.

"Officer Baltasser, would you please tell us what happened on the evening of September 10 of last year."

The officer, dressed in the same smart uniform he had worn the day of the accident, approached the bench. Though his back was to her, he spoke loudly enough that Emma could hear every word.

"Miss Hurst was driving south on the west side of Duke Street, and as she approached the intersection of Fredrick Street, a trolley car stopped to pick up passengers. From the statements of the witnesses, the child with her mother and sister stepped from the curb to board the trolley. The child was a little distance away from her mother when Miss Hurst failed to stop for the trolley, and her automobile knocked the child partially across the intersection."

He turned and looked at Emma briefly.

"I approached Miss Hurst's car and found her with her head resting in her arms on the steering wheel—apparently in shock. The child had been carried by one of the witnesses to the hospital across the street where she died a short time later."

Everyone in the room already knew all this. Both the Intelligencer and the Lancaster New Era had printed elaborate accounts of the accident the day after it had occurred. Still, the details had to be recounted for the official record.

Mr. Brown rose from his seat beside Emma and approached the Bench. She watched as he spanned the space between her table and the judge's bench with confident dignity—like a champion, or an advocate.

"Your Honor, if I may address the court."

Judge Schaeffer nodded.

Mr. Brown began.

"While Miss Hurst held a driver's license for a number of years, she did not drive frequently. This night she was driving four of the Sensenig children to the hospital to visit their father.

"She had come into the city on three or four other occasions, but this time she had a package to be delivered at Mary and Lemon Streets by one of the passengers she had befriended.

"There was an auto on the other side of the trolley tracks, headed south. As she neared Fredrick Street, there was a car parked which obscured her view somewhat, although she saw the tops of the heads of these people. She was looking for a traffic signal from the trolley that the car was going to stop. The auto on the opposite side continued to move and she continued to move, striking the child.

"Miss Hurst has suffered a great deal as the result of this accident. A fair settlement has been made. A very substantial sum has been paid to the parents for the loss of their child.

"There was no great speed on the part of the driver and no violation except at the very last moment, when she possibly should have shown more alertness. But it was a mistake that you or I could have made under the same circumstances, she not being familiar with driving in the city. We believe the ends of justice would well be met if incarceration not be imposed in this case. There was no reckless driving or extreme negligence."

Charles L. Miller, Attorney for the Crill family, rose from his seat to clarify Mr. Brown's statement about there being no violation. "There was a technical violation but no flagrant violation."

Emma started. He was the Crill's lawyer. It sounded more like he was arguing in her defense. She didn't understand.

Judge Schaeffer answered, "Although you say there was no violation and no gross negligence, there nevertheless is a plea of guilty before the court. We cannot ignore that fact."

"May I speak, Your Honor?" It was Officer Baltasser again.

"The police department believes there is a definite violation here. The car Miss Hurst was driving had faulty emergency brakes and she was not strong enough to apply the brakes. Besides, she told us she has been driving 13 years and had never heard anything about stopping for trolley cars. She also said she had never driven in the city before."

Well, he wasn't on her side; that was plain enough. Then again, he was only doing his job.

Attorney Brown spoke up immediately. "Miss Hurst said she had been driving on the street on three or four other occasions."

Officer Baltasser nodded and let the point go.

The Crill's attorney spoke in Emma's defense again. "Miss Hurst has gone out of her way to relieve the suffering of the girl's parents. She offered them her sincerest condolences at the child's viewing, has given them a substantial amount of money—even offered to pay them more as she was able to earn it. They are fully satisfied with these reparations, and it is their wish that she not be sent to jail."

Judge Schaeffer pursed his lips, as if what he was about to say pained him. Then he responded in a serious tone. "The matter before the court is a plea of guilty, and all cases must be treated alike."

Mr. Brown stepped back to where Emma sat and leaned over to whisper in her ear, "Are you absolutely sure you don't want to change your plea? The judge is just waiting for you to ask."

"No, I do not think that would be fair."

Mr. Brown then turned back toward the judge. "Your Honor, my client does not think it would be fair to enter a plea of not-guilty. But there is a question if there is sufficient evidence of gross negligence to justify a conviction by a jury."

What was he saying? That if a jury wouldn't be willing to convict her, a judge shouldn't either?

Apparently, that was exactly what Mr. Brown was implying. Judge Schaeffer leaned across his bench and looked at Emma with compassion. He repeated Brown's question. "Can't you change your plea?"

She knew what he was offering her, a chance for freedom and a clear name. But at what price? A false plea could never give her a clear conscience. She knew she was guilty. God knew. No, she would plead the truth.

Emma squared her shoulders and, with a firmness born of conviction, explained in a strong and resolute tone, "I could; but it wouldn't be the truth."

The judge paused a moment. Then he addressed the room, "Since there is still a plea of guilty before the court," he said, "there is a penalty of ninety days in prison."

Emma Hurst, case number 66, was placed in the custody of the deputy sheriff who mercifully kept his handcuffs on his belt as he shielded her from the press and led her away to prison.

CHAPTER 7

Light in a Dark Place

If the courthouse resembled a Roman temple, the county prison was surely a British castle. The crenellations bordering its two imposing towers seemed more suited to keeping the enemy out than to keeping the residents in. Still, every castle has its dungeon.

Emma's dungeon wasn't as bad as some though. For one thing, it was above ground. For another—it had windows, tall, wide, clear windows—that looked down upon the grassy prison grounds and the city beyond. Of course the windows had bars across them, but she could easily ignore these as long as she kept her focus on the more distant, homier views.

Another nice thing about her dungeon was that everyone had their own bed. And they were not straw-covered pallets but real mattress beds with blankets and pillows.

Seven of the beds had occupants the day Emma entered the cell, seven other women who had case numbers. But these were hardened, earthy women who spoke of unspeakable things with words Emma blushed to hear. They were prostitutes and drunkards, brawlers and thieves whose lives on the streets had made their stay in the Castle seem like a European holiday.

Except for Bertha and Vergie Flowers, case numbers 192 and 193. They seemed more respectable somehow. At least they talked respectably, sprinkling their speech with references to "God's richest blessings" and "Our Lord and Savior," as the situation allowed.

They were a mother and daughter serving two years for stealing jewelry and other items from the home of their employer. Emma didn't quite know what to do with thieves who invoked the Lord's blessings, but she didn't know what to do with a lot of things these days.

"Come on, Dearie, you've shed enough tears on that thing," Mrs. Flowers said as she leaned over and patted Emma's pillow. "Just look at it; you've nearly soaked it right through the case." She sounded like Mom.

Emma looked up at Mrs. Flowers, whose gentle face was framed like a halo by one of the large white light fixtures on the otherwise bare ceiling. "It's just so sad."

"It's a dreadful shame for sure, but the good Lord allowed it to happen and He don't make mistakes."

Emma sat up.

"Come on," Mrs. Flowers continued, as she gently pulled back Emma's covers and helped her out of bed. "Go on over and wash yourself up. And put on some day clothes while you're at it. Nothing makes a woman feel more chipper than putting on a pretty new outfit."

Emma obeyed, taking her best green dress with her to the half-enclosed lavatory that offered the only privacy in the room.

It didn't take her long to change into the clean dress, comb out her long hair, and put it up into a fresh bun; though she could have done a better job if she'd had her hair tonic along. Mrs. Flowers was right. Getting dressed did make her feel better. A little, anyway.

"My, that's a pretty dress for sure," Vergie said when Emma emerged from the lavatory.

"Thank you. It's my Sunday dress. I figured that even if I couldn't get to church, I could still dress like it is a special day."

"Oh we can get to church. Leastways we can go to services. There's a different church sends in a preacher every week. I think the Mennonites are coming today. You don't mind other churches, do you?"

"No, I don't mind. I've been to funerals at other churches before."

"Hey, that's our lunch coming down the hall," one of the women called out as the sound of metal wheels badly in need of oil grew louder beyond their cell door.

Emma picked up her metal dish and joined the other women at the door where each one in turn stuck her dish out through the slit and drew back in a hefty portion of apple dumplings. She added a thick slice of bread and molasses from the perpetual bread table and made a fine meal of it.

When her stomach was full of warm apples and good, solid bread, she borrowed a pen and some paper from Vergie and sat down at the table beneath the windows to write a letter to her family.

. . . .

Greetings to you in the precious name of Jesus our Savior.

This is Sunday morning 11 o'clock. We've just had our noon meal as there is no breakfast served. Supper comes up at 4:30. This morning it was apple dumplings and good too. We actually get all the supper we need. I laid in bed till 10:00 as there is nothing to do anyway.

Would you please send me my fountain pen, Streams in the Desert, bedroom slippers, toilet soap, talcum, my pink seersucker nightgown, blue jay dress, hair tonic, my bottle of ink, crochet hook and thread or embroidery or anything to keep my hands busy. I'll need a laxative too with all this loafing. I could make hairnets too. I'd like my new jacket and my Ohio dress. You won't need to mail these things as I can wait till someone comes in. It's too much to mail anyway.

I can make myself pretty well at home here and time has already put on some speed. Mrs. Flowers would like to have some No. 30 ecru crochet cotton if you have some. She said she'd pay for it. If the girls have some scarves or anything of the sort they'd like to have crocheted, I'll be glad to do it. I suppose you have been to Springville today. The Mennonite church will have services here this afternoon. I am anxious for that.

Who makes the beds since I'm gone? I suppose you don't miss me a whole lot as far as the work is concerned. Mrs. Flowers said she was as happy when she saw me come in here as if I was Jesus, himself. I am surely glad and thankful for Mrs. Flowers' company for I had no idea who I might meet. So we're getting along fine. All of us. I haven't any more news so I will close wishing you all the grace, mercy and peace from our Savior Jesus Christ.

Affectionately,
Emma

There. That was better. She might be trapped in a castle for three months, but no one said she had to be miserable.

. . . .

Emma's family brought her the requested items on the next visitor's day. And they brought more besides: games, books, and goodies enough to share with everyone in her cell.

"Whatcha got there?" asked one of the younger ladies as she peered over Emma's shoulder at all the items in her gift box.

"There is some embroidery thread . . . and yarn. Oh, here's an extra hook. Do you like to crochet?" The woman shook her head.

"What about puzzles? Here is a thousand piece puzzle we can all work on together. Do you like puzzles?" The woman smiled and nodded this time.

Emma dumped the puzzle onto the table and the women all gathered around, glad for something to help pass their lonely hours—all of them, that is, except Helen, who seldom left her corner of the room and ignored the others when she did.

"Helen, my sisters sent us some raisin cookies. Would you care for one?" Emma asked in an effort to coax the antisocial woman to join the group. Helen shook her head. At least she responded.

"I'll take one," said Vergie.

"Oh, yes!" said Emma. "They made them for all of us. Here, pass them around."

Emma lay awake a long time that night, though she did not soak her pillow with tears. She was thinking. The day had been really rather pleasant. What with the puzzle and the rounds of checkers that followed, it had almost been like a Saturday evening back home.

Granted, the company was a little rougher—their language rougher still—but the women had enjoyed one another and the day had actually flown by.

As she lay there with her happy thoughts, Emma heard a rustle from the corner of the room. It was Helen; she was getting out of bed. Now she was tiptoeing over to the puzzle table. What did she want there?

The cookies. She was eating the cookies Esther and Alta had made! Now why would she sneak them alone, in the middle of the night, when she could have eaten them openly with everyone that afternoon?

Not that Emma minded sharing. She had meant it when she had told the ladies to help themselves whenever they wanted, but why did Helen sneak around like a thief? Was theft so much a part of life for Helen that she didn't know any other way to relate to people? Poor girl.

A lot about Emma's cellmates didn't make sense. Like their careless—no, blasphemous—use of the Lord's name. Or their general dislike of men, or their scorn for authority.

She was going to have to be careful, she realized, lest her companions' ways come to seem so normal to her that they no longer seemed shameful. Now that was an appalling thought—that Emma herself could grow so calloused to sin that cursing, scorning, even blaspheming became normal.

She shuddered. If I'm not on my guard, Satan will lead me astray a little at a time. Heavenly Father, guard me and help me to be on guard.

But if Emma was subtly influenced by her cellmates, they were influenced by her as well. Like Mrs. Flowers equating Emma's arrival with the entrance of Jesus into the cell. Wasn't that the way it was supposed to be? Not to be proud or anything, but wasn't Jesus supposed to shine out of His followers like beacons in the night?

Emma had never really thought of herself as a beacon before. Oh, she had tried to be a good example to her siblings, a light in the community and to her co-workers at the garment factory. But she never dreamed she'd end up trying to shine in a prison.

Could God have designed this for her all along? He would not hurt a child; but could He have all along planned that the accident would throw her and these women into the same cell so that He could use her to bring His light into their dark worlds? The thought put a whole new perspective on her sentence.

. . . .

By February, Emma had begun to actually enjoy her days at the Castle. One brisk day, when the grounds were covered with a sparkling white powder, the women were taken out for some fresh air. They giggled like children as they pelted one another with fluffy snowballs and cheered on Emma as she scraped and patted and smoothed a hitherto formless lump of snow into a perfect facsimile of George Washington.

"Well, lookie here, if it ain't the founding father himself!"

"Why that looks just like him! Emma, you should be an artist."

"Oh, it's just a little snowman."

"Yeah, but this one ain't got no carrot for a nose."

"Maybe we should get one. Any of you girls got a carrot in your pocket?"

"I got a piece of old molasses bread."

Slam! A fresh snowball pelted Emma on the neck and the friendly fire began again. A quick passerby would have thought they were a troupe of school girls rather than a gang of convicts.

Spring came, like God promised it always would. George Washington melted into the ground and the snowball wars gave way to peaceful strolls on the prison grounds. Emma had always liked spring, but this year she could almost taste the air; it was so sweet.

Only four days left of her sentence. She wrote a final letter home:

To All the Loved Ones at Home:

"Thanks be unto God, which always causeth us to triumph in Christ" (2 Corinthians 2:14).

Will endeavor to send you a few lines before I'm presented in person. This was surely a perfect spring day. I suppose you have been to Springville. The Presbyterian Church from Paradise was in today, if I didn't misunderstand the announcement.

We had a nice Easter dinner of ham and eggs, potatoes and ice cream.

After visiting hours we go outside until 4:30 and during that time 2 new girls were brought in so there are 6 on our side. Possibilities are that by the time I leave the Flowers will be left to themselves because the rest expect to leave soon.

Poor Mrs. Foust is enduring considerably with her bad leg. I certainly wish I could do something to relieve her. Please remember her in prayer too.

It was so pleasant in the yard this P.M. We sat on the park benches without coats on and enjoyed the beautiful sunlight. We were permitted out right after services, which was at 2:30. And was the most beautiful day I've spent in here.

I received a motto from Mr. and Mrs. Emerson Brubaker and an Easter egg from Katie Martin through the mail yesterday. Had 15¢ due on the Canadian package.

I wrote to Lydia today but to none of the rest, because I can hardly scrape anything together to write.

Tell Ivan I'll soon be there to cut his hair, and to be a good boy. Also Frank and Paul. I'll be so glad to see them all. Somehow I think I could write almost two letters on my homecoming. I'm so childish!

"How blest are they who humbly bow to all God's love allows. Who bravely bear life's hurtful things. Who gladly pay their vows."

God bless and keep you forever.

Your daughter + Sister,

Emma

. . . .

Emma left the Lancaster County Prison on Thursday, April 10, 1947. She had entered guilty, despondent, broken. She emerged free, full of promise, and very much alive. The pain of the accident was still there, of course. It probably always would be. But grief dims with time, and Emma knew that God had somehow used the fading winter to do some very special things in her soul.

CHAPTER 8

At the Crossroads

Emma looked out her bedroom at the serviceable old Plymouth parked in the drive. It was all black of course, even the bumpers.

So much had changed since September; Ivan had grown a bit—if that could be imagined—Mary had wed her longtime sweetheart, John K. Martin, and the Canada geese had flown away and returned again. Emma grabbed her jacket and Bible and forced herself to head down to the car.

They got to the church house much faster than usual. Emma's stomach churned as she stared out at the people standing around in groups, catching up on the week's news before heading in. They were like strangers, or figures on a postcard—far removed from herself and the experiences she had just come through. How could they possibly understand—or know that she was still the same old Emma deep inside?

the exterior of the Martindale church

"Oh, there's Johns!" squealed Ivan.

"Which Johns?" asked Paul.

"Katie's Johns. See? There. Mark and Esther are getting out, and John's got David."

John & Katie with children - Mark, David, Melvin, Esther, and Frank

"Well, Mary's John is here too," added Pop. "Talking with Ivan and Lydia by the hitching post. Sure enough, it's beginning to look like a regular Hurst reunion."

Oh no. The last thing Emma wanted right now was a reunion. Especially not in the parking lot. She hopped out of the car, smiled the way she thought a repentant ex-convict should smile, and made a beeline to the women's entrance.

"Hi, Emma." It was her friend, Clara Martin. "Lovely spring we're having."

"Very lovely."

"Hi, Emma." It was Anna Hoover this time. "It sure is good to have you back."

"Thanks."

The ladies' coatroom was already packed, but Emma managed to hang up her coat and find a seat without too many close encounters.

Not that going inside was much of an escape. Indeed, the meeting room, with its U-shaped section of benches surrounding the central preacher's bench and singer's table, made it impossible to find a seat that was not visible by at least a dozen people.

Emma picked up a songbook and stared at page 52 until the service began. Thankfully, she didn't have to squirm long.

When the service opened and people began to sing, Emma spirits soared. It was like a sound from heaven. She hadn't heard music like that since . . . well, for months, and her heart swelled with the melody that filled the room and resounded from every wall. It was glorious!

Joy lifted her cheeks to her eyes. She couldn't help it. Then she too began to sing from the depth of her soul, with gusto, with joy.

She dared a glance around the room. Everyone smiled in return.

They understood.

Time flowed lazily along for the next few months, and Emma let the current take her where it would. She did some sewing for people, visited Bertha and Vergie Flowers often, and took a correspondence course in commercial art. And she went back to work in the garment factory. That was a mistake.

The sewing that had delighted her as a young twenty-some-thing was now a drudgery. No, it was worse than that, it was detestable. Emma downright hated going to work each day. Slips, slips, slips. How many slips could a person sew in a lifetime? She had lost count.

When she heard that Moses Horning, a chairmaker in Hinkletown, was looking for an artist, she thought perhaps he was the answer to her troubles. He made intricate miniature furniture—desks, rockers, settees, even grandfather clocks—and he wanted her to help paint the tiny pieces. Better yet, she could work in her own sewing room at her own pace.

Emma eagerly examined her first piece—it was a rocking chair, no more than five inches high at the tip of its delicately slatted back. Then she laid newspapers across her desk as a tablecloth and set out her paints, glossy black for the body and white for the accents.

She sang as she painted, first the black, then when that was dry, the white. She could do work like this all day. But there wasn't enough to last all day. In fact, Emma worked so fast that shipments designed to keep her busy for a few weeks were usually finished in just a few days. She was going to have to find something else to fill the rest of her hours. But what?

She took a job with Clara Martin at the telephone company, but she still had several empty hours each evening. She thought she might like to fill them with something significant, something that would leave her at the end of the day feeling like she was better than she had been when she had gotten out of bed. Something, perhaps, along the lines of getting educated.

She had always wished she could study beyond eight grades, but she was the oldest girl, and Mam had needed her at home. That was all changed now. Esther would be marrying Elmer Kurtz in just a few months, so that would be one less mouth to feed, and Alta was plenty capable of helping Mom with the three boys that were left. Besides, the family had gotten along so well without her when she was in jail; she hardly felt they needed her anymore.

She wouldn't have to actually go to the school. She could just get some books and study by herself at home; maybe some math and English. Yes, and a little science to round it all out.

And she would still have plenty of time to keep up her artwork. She had really learned quite a lot from that commercial art course, and she'd hate to see it go to waste. Not to mention, she found it relaxing to sketch and paint on a lazy evening, first the ducks on the pond, then winter scenes with snow blowing across the paper like a gauze curtain, then images of Frank and Paul at work, or Ivan scampering across the lawn with his faith-

Ivan and Buddy pull a cousin.

ful pooch, Buddy. Her sketches were pretty good too; not photograph quality maybe, but good enough that one could easily identify each subject by name.

"You've got quite a talent there, Emma, I won't deny it," Pop said when Emma showed him her latest sketches of Ivan with Buddy. "Still, it's one thing to draw someone who's right across the room from you. The real talent is when you can draw them straight out of your head."

"I do some things out of my head."

"Yeah, but not people. You should be able to draw people out of your head. From memory."

"Why would I do that when they are right there in front of me?"

"Could you draw Mam?"

Emma sat silent for a moment. Mam? She had been gone thirteen years and she had left no photos.

"I'm not exactly sure I can even picture her in my mind, Pop. I mean, I can see her, but in shadows, if you know what I mean."

"Then you might want to get to painting her before she gets so shadowy you don't remember what she looked like at all."

Mam. The younger children probably couldn't picture her. It would be nice to have something for them to remember her by.

Emma went up to her room and made a quick sketch. The outline looked good, at least in a general sort of way, but she wouldn't know for sure till she got some color on the portrait. She got out her oils and brushes and sat down to paint.

She worked for hours, then sat back to survey the emerging face. Something wasn't right with it, but she couldn't figure out what that something was. She ran down to the stripping shed where Pop and the boys were working the tobacco.

"What do you think of this?"

Pop's eyebrows scrunched up thoughtfully as he folded his arms and cupped his chin in his hand. Then he swept his finger in a circle over the painting as if to indicate the general shape of the face. It came to rest above the mouth and cheeks. "No, that's not quite right. Something's wrong, here."

Emma agreed. The bottom of Mam's face was wrong. But what was wrong with it?

She ran upstairs to scrape off some paint and rework the cheeks. Oils are so forgiving.

"Her face wasn't quite that long." Pop said when she returned for another consultation. Yes, that was the problem. She could picture everything about Mam except the lower face. If only Pop could be more descriptive or somehow transfer his mental image of Mam directly into Emma's brain. If only her memory were sharper!

She scraped and repainted again. She strained hour upon hour to recapture an image whose details had begun to slip into the shadows.

Then she sat back and looked. There she was—Mam—looking at her from the portrait in her hands. She took a deep breath and felt her shoulders relax in satisfaction.

"She didn't have such deep eyes," Pop said when Emma showed him the finished painting. But Emma wasn't looking for a critique anymore. She had captured her vision of Mam before it had faded away forever. It was the best work she had ever done.

Emma hung the portrait in the parlor and settled down into her thirties. Months passed, and years. Alta married Stanley Martin. Then Paul married Anna Mary Weaver. And all the while Emma continued to tally up phone bills in the day and study or sketch at night. Surely God expected more from her than this!

Then one day Emma got an idea—a silly one perhaps, but grand. And it came to her from the strangest direction.

Alta and Stanley had stopped in for a visit. Pop and Emma met them at the door.

"Oh, Alta, it has been so lonely around here without you," Emma said. "It's become a house full of men." Pop puffed up his chest and grinned at Stanley. Emma gave Alta a long-suffering look and they all followed Pop into the parlor.

"Ah, here's the old parlor," he said with a quick gesture toward Stanley. "If it had been nicer, I might have had better sons-in-law."

"No, we'd just have more of them," Alta said, deflecting the joke from her husband to Emma. Emma raised her nose in mock dignity and stuck out her tongue as far as it would go.

The banter was fun, but it got her to thinking. She was thirty-five already and she had done nothing to make the world a better place. But what could she do? What could any conservative woman do who had no husband to support or children to raise? The only things she had ever really excelled at were her artwork and her studies. But neither of those did much good for anyone else. Unless...unless just maybe...was there any way that she could be a teacher?

She would have to get a real high school diploma—that would mean a full year as a resident at the high school—and then she would need a teacher's certificate after that. That would mean four years away at college.

Emma at the gate by the homeplace.

Ach, Emma, college is a dangerous place; our kind of people don't go there. Besides, you are too old. Do you think you're going to sit down and study with students who are barely half your age? Sheepishly she brought the idea up to Mom.

"Emma," Mom said with her wonderful mix of confidence and encouragement, "you can do everything you set your mind to." Then her cheeks rose to her twinkling eyes. "Except get a man."

CHAPTER 9

A New Direction

Emma moved her trowel with broad, sweeping motions and set it beside her on the grass. The cement had a warm earthy smell, the smell of summer, and of bare feet, and of home.

There, that was the last section of the stairs. Now it would be easy for everyone to walk down to the mailbox to get her letters—and to post letters to her in return. Lancaster Mennonite High School (LMHS) was much farther away than she had always imagined it was.

The steps Emma built to the mailbox.

She cordoned off the wet slab in a way that clearly said to any passing boy or dog, "Keep out!" She was pretty sure Ivan would get the message. She wasn't too sure about Buddy, though.

Then again, maybe Ivan was the one she should worry about. It was he, after all, who had coaxed the poor, faithful dog to get into a basket and ride with him to the top of the silo. Not that he had set out to have an adventure. Adventures just sort of caught Ivan unawares.

He had watched each autumn with envy as the heavier men in the family rode up the silo in the elevator Pop had rigged in the attached chute. It was really nothing more than a cable slung over a contrived pulley with a wooden plank for a seat on one end and a metal counterweight on the other.

The counterweight was just heavy enough to give a 160-200 pound man a nice slow ride to the top so he wouldn't have to climb the ladder. Ivan did not weigh 160 pounds. He barely weighed a hundred. But he and Buddy together—now that might just be enough weight to do the trick.

Of course Buddy wasn't about to sit on a wooden plank, so Ivan tied a basket to the plank and somehow persuaded the dog to get in. Then he wriggled in beside Buddy, released the cable from its restraining latch, and beamed with satisfaction as the basket began to rise.

Ah, this is what it's like to be one of the big guys, to work hard and have a weight do your climbing for you.

But Ivan was only half a big guy, so when his canine half had the sense to jump out of the basket at the last possible moment, the boy was subject to the forces of a counterweight that was nearly twice his size.

He shot into the air like a bullet, his heart pounding as he looked up and saw the circle of sky at the top of the chute grow larger by the second. He clutched the cable and prayed faster than it takes a .22 to hit a squirrel. Just when it seemed that discharge was inevitable, his body lurched and he came to a jarring halt just inches from the top of the pulley—and the open sky beyond.

Pop, in his foresight had rigged it so that the counterweight struck the ground well before the seat could rise high enough to strike the pulley. Ivan was saved!

Emma laughed at the memory. She was going to miss her little brother when she was at school.

Ach, Emma, why the mixed emotions? Classes are only held on weekdays. You will be home every weekend. Besides, you are going to a real high school. And after that? Well, we will just have to wait and see.

. . . .

"Well, Miss Hurst," said Amos Weaver, the principal at LMHS, "it looks like you have really applied yourself. Your studies at home are equivalent to three years of high school credit. You only need four more credits to graduate.

"Unfortunately, all of those are social studies credits. That would be like eating potatoes for breakfast, dinner, and supper. You need some variety. Why not take pre-professional tests for two of these courses—I'm sure you'll pass them— and take two other classes to round things out?"

"That sounds like a good idea."

"How about Typing and Bookkeeping? They are practical courses, and those skills may come in useful for a woman in the workforce. If you add World History & Problems in Democracy and American History & Civics, you'll have a well-rounded year."

. . . .

Emma thought back to the conversation with Mr. Weaver as she set her bag on the desk and looked around the dorm room. It was a lot like her room back home, only there were two of everything: two desks, two beds, two dressers. One bed was already littered with boxes.

It's going to be strange living and studying with another person for a year. Oh well, it can't be any stranger than trying to live like a Christian in a cell full of street women.

Her thoughts were interrupted by the sound of someone entering the room. It was a young lady, maybe Alta's age, in a blue dress with a matching belt.

"Hi, you must be Emma." The girl smiled and held out her hand.

"Yes. And you are Mabel Stauffer?"

"Mm-hm."

"I see you are already settled in."

"I don't live too far from here."

"Me either," Emma said. "In fact, I plan to go home on weekends."

"Me too. You seen the campus yet?"

"Not fully."

"Come on. I'll show you around and we can have lunch together."

Emma set her bag down and followed Mabel out of the room. She could unpack later.

It was a good thing she had gone with Mabel that first day because school started just a couple of days later, and Emma found that she spent most of her time at her desk, tabulating columns, writing papers, typing assignments, and studying for hours upon end.

She did not write as many letters home as she had anticipated. Perhaps it was because school work occupied so much of her evenings. Or perhaps it was because her weekends at home were sufficient for keeping the family room in her heart full. More likely though, it was because Emma was on the road to her future, and she was finding the journey full enough.

Emma graduated from high school on May 28, 1954. She was thirty-six years old.

CHAPTER 10

From the Past to the Future

The New York skyline stood out in sharp contrast to the darkening sky beyond, then disappeared as the sun slowly slipped below the horizon. Emma leaned over the rail of the ocean liner and took in the sight with silent wonder.

She hadn't gone to college immediately after graduating from high school like she had thought she might. She had needed time to think and to pray, and to make sure she was doing the right thing. It made no sense to rush into a future without God, and she hadn't discerned His will yet. She would need to wrestle a bit longer.

"What do you think, Pop?" she had asked when she heard about a trip to Mennonite Europe and the Holy Land beyond. "Should I go?"

"Emma, if I could fit in your suitcase, I'd go along. It's the chance of a lifetime. Don't miss it."

So here she was, leaning over the rail of the Queen Elizabeth as it steamed into the lands of her spiritual past, where she hoped to find some direction for her future.

The salty, vibrant smell of the sea followed her inside as she left the promenade in search of Mary Weaver and Sadie Harder. These two were her traveling mates in the troupe of twenty-five Mennonites, scattered amongst the crowd on a ship that could hold over two thousand. To Emma's Martindale eyes it seemed like she had passed three times that many people already!

The ship was massive—like a floating city—with shops, libraries, cinemas, and an endless maze of corridors that all looked very much the same. She finally found her mates, or rather, they finally found each other in and around the cluster of staterooms that would be their floating home for the next five days.

After supper, which was eaten with more utensils than Emma quite knew what to do with, the group retreated to the quiet of their rooms and bunked down for the night.

Who would have ever imagined that Emma Hurst, farm girl from eastern Pennsylvania, would be bobbing upon the water like a strider on the pond. Only this wasn't a pond, it was the Atlantic Ocean, and its ripples were more like monstrous hills of water that left her stomach hanging in mid-air with each drop into the gaping troughs.

"Oh, I don't think I could bear to even look at the breakfast table," said Mary to Emma and Sadie the next morning."

Sadie nodded. "It's these swells. Half the group is in bed, I hear. And none of them wants breakfast."

"I think the crew expected something like this," added Emma, "at least judging from the menu. Breakfast isn't until 11 and it's just a bit of hot soup and toast."

"Well, I don't want even that!"

The three women went up to sit on their deck chairs until the rolling of the ship drove them below where they could sleep off the torment in relative privacy.

The following days brought calmer seas, and the group enjoyed a relaxing mix of wave-watching, dining, and worshiping together in the small cinema in their section of the ship.

They disembarked in Southampton, England, on Wednesday, October 19, 1955, no worse for wear, except, perhaps, that they walked with their legs spread unnaturally wide as though in anticipation of a sudden attack from a rolling wave.

England was a lot like the States in many ways, although it was damper and older, and simultaneously statelier, yet more rustic, if that can be explained. Not to mention that it would have been impossible to hide the ruinous remains of WWII bombing raids that still dotted the countryside.

But of all the things Emma experienced in the country that gave birth to the United States, the most exciting was seeing the Queen.

They had heard a rumor that she would be leaving Buckingham Palace for tea the very morning they were scheduled to view it. As they stood beside a fountain in the raincoats they had come to consider necessary attire in this land of perpetual drizzle, they spotted a motorcade of majestic-looking vehicles parading out from the inner court through high, wrought-iron gates. The Queen!

They smiled and waved, pointing first to this car then to that; more sure with each passing vehicle that they had indeed seen Her Majesty. As they returned to the bus in delight, their guide, John Coffman, ran toward them gesturing. That was only the Queen's sister.

They dashed back to their posts beside the fountain and smiled with deep satisfaction when a Rolls Royce, bearing the royal insignia, passed right before their eyes. Smiling and waving from within was the royal majesty herself, Elizabeth II, the Queen of England!

But for all its excitement, their fleeting view of the monarch paled before their experiences across the Channel in the Netherlands and Switzerland—the cradle of Dutch Anabaptism.

"I can hardly believe we are actually in the land of the first Mennonites," Emma said to Sadie and Mary.

"And all those martyrs," added Mary. "Can you imagine?"

They couldn't imagine—until they stood on the bank of the Limmat River in Zurich, where Felix Manz, the first Mennonite martyr, had been trussed up like a chicken and tossed into the middle of the river.

"It's such a holy place," Sadie said. "Can't you just feel the sacredness of what he did?"

"Do you suppose this is the exact spot where they tied him up and put him in the boat?" asked Mary.

"Or where his mother stood?" added Sadie. "I can hardly bear to think of her watching—actually shouting, Don't give in, Felix! Stay faithful to the end! "

Mary looked teary-eyed. "Can you imagine a mother being able to do that? I could never be that strong. I'd probably run away and hide."

Emma bowed her head. Felix had been only twenty-nine years old when he died. Emma was nearly forty. What would she have done in his place?

The voice of Gideon Yoder, their tour director, broke into the women's conversation. "I think it would be fitting to have a season of prayer. Brother John, will you lead us please?"

After John had led in a moving prayer to the God who had been by Felix's side, Gideon softly began to sing. The rest of the group joined in, softly, reverently, personally:

> Faith of our fathers, living still,
> In spite of dungeon, fire and sword;
> O how our hearts beat high with joy
> When e're we hear that glorious Word!
>
> Faith of our fathers! Holy Faith!
> We will be true to thee till death!
> – Frederick W. Faber 1849

Till death. Emma had tried to be true. But to death? And how about to life? Felix's mother had to be true and yet still live. Perhaps that was the harder task. Oh, Father, Emma prayed with all her soul. I would be true to Thee till death—and to life too. But I am too weak and not able. Make me able. And may only Thy will, and not mine, be done in my life.

The group wound their way through the Alps, finally descending to the Italian peninsula where they saw the many cathedrals in Milan, Pisa, and Rome. But none of those imposing centers of worship, despite their magnificent architecture and gilded ornamentation, affected Emma as had that echoing spot beside the Limmat River.

They took off from Rome in a TWA Constellation on the evening of Thursday, November 11. It was Emma's first time in the air and she found it exhilarating. As they left the lights of Rome twinkling on the ground beneath them, she was overwhelmed by the thought that she was, in many ways, traveling back in time.

They landed first in Egypt, land of the pyramids, sphinxes, and camels.

Emma had always wanted to ride a camel.

She stood against a palm tree and watched a few of the others mount the beasts. First John, then Gideon, then Sadie. It didn't look too hard, just straddle the animal at the neck, scooch up onto the back, and hold on as the animal rises, first on its hind legs then on its front.

"You going to ride?" It was Mary.

"It's either that or take a horse and buggy. I could do that at home! What about you?"

"I'll brave it if you do."

Emma stepped forward and was told by her driver that she would be riding on a camel named Whiskey. Well, that would be a first.

She straddled the camel's neck and scooched up on the blanket as she had seen the others do. It was easy as cake. Then the beast started to rise.

Its hind quarters rose to such a height behind her that she could not help but slide back down onto its neck. She now understood why the handgrip was placed where it was—to keep her from slipping completely over the camel's head to the ground beyond.

When the front legs finally rose to match the back legs, Emma heaved a grateful sigh and resumed her place on the blanket.

Alighting from the furry mounts was more a test of dexterity than getting on, for before she could get a firm hold on the grip and steady herself for the descent, the beast collapsed his front legs and dropped to the ground, nearly hurling her to the sand in the process. Emma suspected they sat down that way just to get back at the humans for making them take the same dusty walk day after day.

. . . .

Emma found herself in another desert a few days later. She was on the road to Damascus, and this time she was seated in a car. When she crested the last hill in the Lebanon Mountains and overlooked the plain, she was stunned by the contrast. Instead of the barren, rocky wilderness that had bordered the road from the Mediterranean to Syria, there was a river. Around it, flourishing like an oasis, was Damascus, the white jewel of the desert.

Could this be the place where Saul had met the Lord? No, that must have been on a more southerly road. Still, the view must have been quite similar.

And the street called Straight—where Paul had pondered that encounter for three days—was still there. Of course, it had probably looked quite different back then, but she felt the thrill of standing where had Paul stood, seeing the places he saw! Oh that God would also appear to her in a vision, to say to her in a clear voice, This is the way; walk ye in it.

But maybe it didn't work that way anymore—or for most people at least. Maybe God just let normal circumstances roll back and forth through a person's life and their job was just to make sure each individual day was lived in a way that pleased Him.

She wrestled with these thoughts for the rest of the trip—from the overlook on Mt. Nebo, to the banks of the Jordan, across the hills at Bethlehem, all the way to the shores of Galilee.

And then she got to Golgotha. As she stood beside the empty tomb and shared Communion with the friends she had come to love so well over the past few weeks, she finally understood. And she sang it from the depth of her will:

> My richest gain I count but loss; and pour
>   contempt on all my pride . . .
> That were a present far too small . . .
> Love so amazing, so divine, demands my soul,
>   my life, my all.
> – Isaac Watts, 1707

Emma knew what she needed to do with her future. She needed to crucify it and let God bring to life the plans He knew were best. She would work at the telephone company until she saved up enough money for her tuition, then she would let God decide if she should go to college or not.

CHAPTER 11

Higher Education

Pop gave that little cough of his that signaled the end of the silent prayer. Mom, Ivan, and Emma looked up.

As Pop spread butter, then jelly, on his bread, he looked at Emma and asked, "Have you given any more thought to what you want to do with your life? Not that we're itching for you to leave, but with Frank married off to Anna Mary, I thought maybe you'd be thinking about college again or something."

"I have enough for the tuition; I'm just not sure if God wants me to go or not."

"Do you think He wants you to be a teacher?"

"Yes."

"How else will you get to be a teacher if you don't go and get your teacher's degree?"

"It's just that no one from our conference has gone to college—at least none of the women—and I'm not sure what they would think."

"They'd think you did what God wanted you to do. Emma, everyone knows you're a scholar. They could hardly want you to sit around doing nothing when you could be teaching their young'uns to read and write."

"I don't think it's the teaching she's worried about," said Mom, "but the years at college."

"It's not like she's a rebellious young gad-about, said Pop."

Emma chuckled. "No, I'm certainly not that." Then she sobered again. "I'm worried about the seizures, too."

"You haven't had a seizure in years," Pop said.

"No, but life's been pretty laid back."

"Ach, you'll never do anything if you're always worrying about what might be. God gave you the funding. He gave you the brains. And He gave you the dream. I say do it and make it happen."

So it was settled.

.　.　.　.　.　.　.　.　.　.　.　.　.　.　.

Emma set her bag on the desk and looked around the dorm room with a strange sense of familiarity. It was a lot like her room at the high school: a pair of matching beds, a pair of desks, and a pair of dressers. If it weren't for that strangely-curved mountain out the western window, she'd have thought she was back at LMHS. But this wasn't high school; it wasn't even Pennsylvania. It was Eastern Mennonite College (EMC) in Harrisonburg, Virginia.

"Hi. You must be Emma." Emma turned around as a smart-looking woman walked into the room with a bag on each arm. She set them on the bed and held out her hand.

Emma offered hers in return. "Yes, fresh from Pennsylvania.

And you are . . .?"

"Agnes Schaeffer, fresh from Nigeria."

"Africa?"

"Yep. I was serving in the missions there, but thought I'd better come back and get some more training in cooking and sewing, that sort of thing; so I signed up for home economics."

Emma cringed. "I fear my story is much more mundane."

"What are you here for?"

"Elementary education. It's required for teachers in Pennsylvania."

"I could never be a teacher. Don't have the brains for it."

"Oh, I'm sure you could."

"Which side do you want?"

"Of the room? Oh, I don't mind either. Do you have a preference?"

"Either's fine with me too. Since you already have your bags there, why don't you take that side and I'll take this one."

The women had been unpacking and organizing their things for a while when Emma asked, "Have you ever seen someone have a seizure?"

"You mean like epilepsy? No, why?"

"Well, I used to have seizures during the night sometimes, mostly when I was under a lot of stress."

"Do you still get them?"

"I haven't for several years."

"Should I do something if you have one?"

"No, they wear themselves out. I just didn't want you to worry if something happened."

"Thanks for the warning."

And a timely warning it was. By mid-September Emma was tired from staying up late to study. By early October she was wearing down from too much thinking. By mid-October, when she and her classmates were recovering from the worst flu outbreak since the 1920's, she crashed. She was still off medication, and the seizure was a big one.

. . . .

There was no keeping the seizure a secret from the campus physician; Emma lived in a dorm, after all. Agnes at the very least knew what had happened, and the six or so women in the adjoining rooms and across the hall could hardly have failed to hear her banging in the night.

"I'm sorry, Miss Hurst, but you will need to go back on medication," Dr. Eshleman said.

"I can't concentrate when I'm on it; my mind gets so sluggish."

"You can't function without it—at least not as long as you intend to keep studying so hard."

Emma took the pills, but it was as she had feared. She had trouble rousing in the morning, felt drowsy during afternoon classes, and positively could not concentrate on her evening studies. How would she ever pass her courses like this? Besides, she had made a commitment to leave everything to God. Was she going to back out on that now?

She secretly weaned herself of the medicine like she had those many years before, one sliver at a time, but she also forced herself to get to bed at a reasonable hour. By the time the semester was over, she was medication-free again.

The second semester was harder than the first. There was no way she could possibly get to bed early and still get all A's. She made it to May and final exams week. Then she seized again.

Seized or was seized? Emma began to wonder if she really had epilepsy after all. What if her real problem was that she was possessed like the poor boy in the Gospel of Luke? What if she wasn't even really a Christian!

"That's a lie from the pit!" said Agnes when Emma confided her fears to her in the privacy of their dorm room. "Demons can't possess Christians."

"But what if I'm not really a Christian?"

"I can't believe you'd even think such a thing! I've never met anyone as in touch with God as you are."

"How do you know I'm not just living a lie?"

"Oh, Emma, you can't live with a person day in and day out and not know what kind of person they are."

"Then why does this keep happening?"

"Have you asked God to take it away?"

"Yes."

"When?"

"When I first got them."

"And did you have enough faith to believe He would?"

"Well. . ."

"Let's pray again—now that your faith is stronger."

Agnes sat beside Emma on the bed and put her arm around her shoulders. Then she began to pray.

"Father," Agnes said aloud—as if the Listener were right there in the room with them—"we know You are able to do anything and we ask You to put Your healing hand on Emma and take away all seizures if it's not against Your will. In any case, please comfort her with an absolute assurance of Your love for her and her position as one of Your children."

Emma joined in, "Heavenly Father, if I can glorify Thy name with these seizures, then let it be so. Let Thy will be done and not mine. And beyond anything else, I want Thy salvation. Please make me clean and whole. In the precious name of Jesus."

"Amen."

A calmness settled over Emma. She really was a Christian. She knew that for sure now. She knew too that God would heal her if it was His will to do so. And if it wasn't? Then it would be her will to surrender.

Emma passed all her exams without another seizure.

. . . .

Summer fled by and Emma found herself sitting in the EMC chapel where college president John R. Mumaw was captivating the students with his nightly lectures on the third chapter of Colossians. How could he speak on the same chapter night after night and hold their attention? Several students had already made confessions or rededicated themselves to God.

"If ye then be risen with Christ," he said with enthusiasm, "seek those things which are above, where Christ sitteth on the right hand of God. Set your affection on things above, not on things on the earth. For ye are dead, and your life is hid with Christ in God" (Colossians 3:1-3).

If you are what you say you are, if you have crucified your natural self with all its sin, pride, and personal ambition, if you are truly risen to new life in Christ, then rise up! Throw off the lowly things of this passing existence and strive for the things that will last!

Emma's soul thrilled at the call. To rise above herself—to leave behind Emma Hurst with all her petty ambitions and pride. Oh, that was what she wanted!

"Put on therefore, as the elect of God, holy and beloved, bowels of mercies, kindness, humbleness of mind, meekness, long-suffering; forbearing one another, and forgiving one another, if any man have a quarrel against any: even as Christ forgave you, so also do ye" (Colossians 3:12, 13).

– he quoted the next night.

Again she was gripped.

How often had she been unmerciful or self-centered—toward Pop, toward Ivan, toward her classmates? That is not the way a risen-again person acts; not if they are filled with the Spirit of Christ, and Emma knew for certain now that she was indeed filled with that Spirit.

"And whatsoever ye do in word or deed, do all in the name of the Lord Jesus, giving thanks to God and the Father by him" (Colossians 3:17).

– he concluded.

Whatsoever. That meant everything. She was to do everything for Jesus. And not with the sort of perfection born of human effort and pride—like getting all A's because she studied hard—but with the perfection that comes from doing something for Christ and by His power.

Emma made her own private confession to God that week. Not only was she going to set her mind on things above and try to do everything for Christ; she was also going to memorize the entire third chapter of Colossians—by God's power of course—so that she did not forget where to focus her life.

Her new commitment was tested by one of the youngish fellows who greeted her each day with a smirky, "Hi, Grandma."

Before the Mumaw revivals—that is, before her own revival—she would have just pretended not to notice. But that was neither forbearing in meekness nor longsuffering; it was just ignoring. Surely she could love the boy better than that. The next time she saw him, things would be different.

"Hi, Grandma," the boy said when they passed on the sidewalk the next morning.

Emma lifted her head with a childish grin and replied in kind. "Hello, Sonny."

The boy looked at her in astonishment. Then his eyes met hers and they both laughed.

Emma and Mr. Sonny continued to greet one another when they passed on the quad, each knowing that in the other they had found a friend.

She found her Colossians commitment tested again when she passed by her parked car one morning on the way from her dorm to the dining hall. Long before she was close enough to read the license plate, she had reason to doubt that the black '48 Plymouth parked at the curb was actually hers for, unlike any other car in the Weaverland Conference, this one had a bumper that had been painted fire-engine red.

This wasn't just a spunky, Hi Grandma; it was a malicious, spiteful act of vandalism. It was also a slap at her conference and the conservative traditions they held dear. It was hard to feel merciful, forgiving, or forbearing in any way.

The words of Colossians rose up like a song to soothe and instruct her. ". . . if any man have a quarrel against any: even as Christ forgave you, so also do ye." Other verses she had memorized as a child joined the chorus. Love your enemies. Turn the other cheek. Return good for evil. What good did it do to memorize the words if she didn't put them into practice?

Well, she didn't know who had done the horrendous paint job, so she couldn't exactly return good for evil. She could turn the other cheek though. She could leave the bumper red and continue to park the car out by the road where it would be easy for the vandal to apply even more of his ugly, disrespectful artwork. It sounded crazy! But the idea made her smile.

Alas! Emma wasn't the only Bible-living person on campus. The sympathetic maintenance man, having noticed the bumper, painted over the brilliant red with a dull, flat black. Now Emma could not only not turn the other cheek to the vandal, but she had to drive around with a bumper that looked like she was too cheap to have it painted properly.

Ach, Emma! Sometimes it is harder to live out the gospel than it is to commit to it in your head.

Emma's senior picture at collage

CHAPTER 12

Going it Alone

Nineteen sixty-one was a momentous year. Yuri Gagarin became the first man in space, John F. Kennedy became the 35th President of the United States, and Emma Hurst became the second-grade teacher at the Union Grove Elementary School. Of the three, Emma was undoubtedly the most terrified.

She parked her car and stared at the building. It was brand-new, a monument to the spirit of integration and consolidation that was sweeping the nation, with eight separate classrooms surrounding a central common area where students would have easy access to the restrooms, health office, and combination gym/auditorium/dining-room in the rear of the building.

It wasn't a bad design overall, but the front of the building was unlike anything Emma had ever seen. Oh, there were the nicely trimmed doors that one expects in the front of a school, but you couldn't see them from the parking lot because they were hidden behind a monstrous, pale blue, freestanding boiler room that spanned the entire middle section of the building. Gardening around the thing must have been a landscaper's nightmare. At least the canopy-covered walkways surrounding the tower made it almost appear that the structure was an attached part of the main building. Still, canopies couldn't change the fact that the boiler was so far from the rear of the building that the water in the pipes cooled before they could heat the remotest rooms.

. . . .

"Miss Hurst?" whispered a voice from just outside Emma's classroom door. It was Mrs. Weaver, the first-grade teacher. She was dressed in a smart-looking skirt and blouse like all the other teachers at Union Grove. All the others, except Emma, that is.

"You'll never make it in that public school with your old-fashioned dress and prayer covering," the nay-sayers and joy-stealers had warned her repeatedly when they had found out that she planned to teach at Union Grove. "You just watch and see."

Well, they had been wrong. Emma's colleagues treated her with the same respect and kindly manner in which they treated everyone else. Mrs. Weaver even looked up to her as a sort of role model.

Emma stepped into the hallway just far enough that she could talk with Mrs. Weaver while still keeping an eye on the thirty-five seven-year-olds working quietly at their desks.

"What is it?"

"Our room is freezing again. The children have their jackets on, and some of them are still shivering. Would you mind terribly if we came in here? Just for the morning, until the room warms up."

"Of course you may. We can easily divide the room in half and pretend we are back in the old one-room school."

"Thanks."

Oh dear, thought Emma when Mrs. Weaver left. However will we finish our lessons now? And we are already so far behind.

"Children," she said in the teacher's voice she had learned at college. "Children, Mrs. Weaver's students will be joining us again this morning. We will have to be extra quiet so they can concentrate on their work.

"Come, let's squeeze our desks toward the back so they can have the blackboards.

"Samuel, will you and Rachel please tidy up the counter there? Thank you.

"Patricia, you may wash the blackboard. Hurry now, they will be here in just a minute."

Nothing in her classes at EMC had prepared Emma for anything like this. It was hard enough that her own students were on five different reading levels, but first-graders? They still sounded every word out loud!

Fortunately, the first grade room had warmed up by lunchtime, so Emma and her students had their room to themselves the entire afternoon, though they still found it hard to concentrate.

When the children were dismissed, Emma sat down at her desk with a sigh. Both hands trembled as she opened her lesson book to Tuesday, October 10. She was three days behind.

. . . .

"Well, if it isn't Miss Hurst," said the doctor holding out a friendly hand when she went to see him the following week. "It's been a while. How are the seizures?"

"Actually, I've been seizure-free for three and a half years now."

"So what brings you in?"

"Well, I'm a bit ashamed to admit it, but I think maybe I might be having a case of nerves."

"Has anything changed recently: a move, change in jobs, death in the family?"

"I have started a new job. I'm teaching at the Union Grove Elementary School. Second grade. The students are well-behaved and I enjoy the work, but I just can't seem to finish everything before the day ends."

"Maybe you're trying too hard."

"Teaching is an important job."

"All jobs are. But if I know you, Emma. You are trying to do a perfect job. Any physical symptoms?"

"My hands shake sometimes."

"How are you sleeping?"

"All right, when I finally get to it. There is so much to do in the evenings."

"And this hasn't brought on any seizures?"

"No."

"Not even little ones?"

"None. The fact is, a friend prayed for me after a bad spell and I haven't felt a thing since. I really believe I might be healed for good."

"That would be wonderful. Still, you're under a lot of stress. How would you feel about going on a little medication?"

A decidedly Hurst look began to take shape on Emma's pursing lips and narrowing eyelids.

"Not seizure medicine," the doctor quickly added, "just something to calm your nerves a bit."

"Will it make me drowsy?"

"It shouldn't."

"Then I think I'd like to try it."

The tranquilizers worked immediately. Emma's hands stopped shaking and she was able to sleep better. But they didn't do much for her emotions. The trouble was, the calmer she got, the more she was able to see what a poor job she was doing.

Teacher?—ha! You can't even make it to Christmas without medicine. Your students fall more and more behind with each unfinished day. Maybe you should quit fooling yourself and go back to sewing slips.

But Emma was a teacher, and she was a very normal one—as she found out the day she visited the second grade class at the nearby Blue Ball School.

"I was inspired by the way you handled your class," she said to the teacher there. "Especially the way you calmly dealt with that disruptive boy and still completed your lesson plans. You obviously have things under firm control."

The teacher chuckled. "Finished my lessons! We are a week behind, if not more."

"What will you do when you get to the end of the year?"

"Thank God for all His help and start planning for next year."

"Are you serious?"

"Sure. A person can only do so much; and children seldom perform according to the way we plan."

"I'll confess, I haven't approached my teaching that way at all."

"If you don't, you won't survive."

Ach! Emma was doing it again! Trying to conquer the world by her own power—her own piddly, insignificant strength. Would she never learn?

The year went much better after that. The years that followed were better still, and Emma made a fine teacher after all. Oh, she still had her little crises, times when she tried too hard—or tried too hard not to try hard—but they grew less frequent with each new class. God didn't expect Emma to be perfect. He never had.

CHAPTER 13

The Man at the Green Dragon

Pop received the bowl of mashed potatoes from Mom, slapped a spoonful onto his plate, and passed them to Emma. There were only the three of them at the table since Ivan married Mary Martin last November. When he left, Pop, Mom, and Emma had moved into the smaller Dawdi house so Paul and Anna Mary could have the main part of the house for themselves and their five little ones.

"I had the strangest conversation at the Green Dragon the other day," said Pop.

"With whom?" asked Emma.

"Old Aaron Hoover."

Mom looked at Pop queerly. "I'd hardly call Aaron old. He can't be more than fifty-five."

"He's a widower, and it's practically the same thing."

"What did you talk about?" asked Emma.

"Well now, that was the odd thing. He told me he wants to date one of my daughters."

Emma cocked her head. "But they're all married."

"Not all of them."

Emma stared at her father, realization dawning as she read his face. "You mean he asked to date me?"

"That's what he said."

Emma looked down and stirred her potatoes. When she looked up, Pop was munching away on a pork chop as if they had been discussing the top price for corn at the Green Dragon.

"What did you tell him?"

"I told him he was confusing grief with loneliness, what with Lizzie being gone only a few months."

"What did you say about me?"

"You? I told him you were a scholar, and he probably wouldn't like dating a girl with more brains than himself."

"You didn't!"

"Not in so many words. But you've got to admit it, the two of you aren't exactly a matched set. Besides, he's practically old enough to be your father."

"Only ten years older," said Emma.

"Hmph."

Mom leaned back in her chair and crossed her arms. "Now, Frank, if I recall correctly, you are eleven years older than me. Does that make you old enough to be my father?"

"That's beside the point. My children needed a mother. Aaron's are all grown."

"Are you saying you married me only for my maternal qualities?"

"Don't go twisting my words, Esther. That was entirely different, and you know it."

"Would you let me date him if I wanted to?" asked Emma.

"You mean you'd actually consider it?"

"I might."

"Well, I'll be."

A date. With a man. It had been nearly thirty years since Emma had been on a date, back when her suitors were still considered boys. But Aaron Hoover was no boy. He was a father—a grandfather! It would be like dating a family. Still . . .

. . . .

Emma's right index finger tapped out a tattoo on the windowsill. All she could see beyond the light by the silo was a hazy silhouette indicating that, somewhere out in that inky blackness, there was an orchard and a lane that led to it from the back of the property. She should have seen Aaron's headlights by now.

She was relieved he had decided to come in the back way. Everyone in the neighborhood would recognize him by his black Rambler. Especially Paul. Snoopy "little" brother. Now wouldn't he like to know why Aaron Hoover was calling at nine o'clock on a Sunday evening? Well, let him wonder.

"Hey! Who's that out there?" yelled a voice from somewhere outside. It sounded like Paul's.

Emma ran to the side of the house and opened the door. Her brother had the upstairs window open and was leaning out, calling to a man who was walking up the driveway. Behind him was a black Rambler.

"Say, who are you, and what do you want this time of the night?"

Aaron continued to walk toward the front door as though he hadn't heard Paul. Paul slammed the window shut. Emma was sure she heard her brother walk down the stairs, but he never entered the room.

Her grin spread from her mouth all the way up to the corners of her eyes as she greeted her visitor. "I imagine that was not exactly the sort of welcome you expected."

"Not exactly." Aaron saw Emma's expression and couldn't help smiling with her. He took off his hat and bowed lightly. "May I come in before someone else opens a window?"

"I would be honored."

She led the way to the parlor and offered him a seat in the stuffed chair.

"I thought you were going to come in the orchard lane."

"I was planning to. But they're doing some roadwork back there, and I couldn't make it over the dirt heaped up against your lane. Nearly got stuck as it was, so I figured I might just as well pull right up front. I really didn't mind except for . . ."

"Except for Paul." They laughed together, but quietly this time, lest Paul should get more information than he was entitled to.

"Pop tells me you two talked about me at the market," said Emma from the chair opposite Aaron's. "I'd love to know what you said."

"Well, I was a bit nervous, as you can imagine. I didn't know what he'd think and all. So I beat around the bush a good bit."

"He told me that he told you he thought you were confusing grief with loneliness, and it was too soon to start dating."

"He what?!" Aaron leaned forward in his chair like a conspirator and whispered to Emma. "If you could have heard him, Emma, you'd have laughed as hard as I wanted to."

She leaned forward as if to join the conspiracy, then begged with her expression for him to tell her more. He clasped his hands in his lap and looked at the carpet a moment. Then he looked her in the eyes.

"You know how much I loved Lizzie," he began, somewhat hesitantly. "She was everything to me. I told Frank, er, your Pop, how much I was missing her and asked what he thought about me dating someone. I remembered how soon he had started dating Esther when your mother passed away, so I figured he'd understand. You know, if it was too soon or not.

" 'Too soon!' he says. 'A man can't live with a dead lady! No, Aaron,' he says, 'You need to get out.'

"But when I told him it was you I was thinking to date, his tune changed.

" 'Isn't it rather soon?' he says to me then."

Emma's jaw dropped. "He didn't!"

"Yes, Ma'am. He did."

"Well, I'll be."

"Do you think it's too soon?"

"Aaron, if I thought it was too soon for you to date, I would not have agreed to see you. No, I don't think it's too soon for either of us. I think the time is just right."

Emma floated through the next few weeks. When she read her Bible in the morning, Aaron seemed to speak from every page. When she looked out over her classroom in the afternoon, Aaron sat in every desk. When she tried to correct papers in the evening, every word seemed to whisper, Aaron.

It was worse at church, for Aaron was one of the song leaders. She couldn't even look at the preacher without seeing Aaron sitting—and pretending to concentrate—at the singer's table.

The song leader's table at the Martindale church

Did everyone see the way he looked at her? The way he beamed when she looked up, or fumbled as he flipped pages in a vain attempt to find a suitable song? Surely they must.

But when he asked her to marry him, her heart slammed into a brick wall. She loved Aaron, of that she was sure, but she loved teaching too. How could she give up teaching when there was so little for her to do, childless, at home?

"I don't want you to stop teaching, Emma," Aaron said when she confessed what was troubling her. "Between working at the car wash and hauling Amish or supplies for Stevie, I'm gone all day anyway."

"But I have paperwork almost every evening."

"I know that. You could do it at the kitchen table, and I could do my things right beside you, and we could be together even as we work."

"What about housework? I wouldn't be able to keep house like Lizzie did. Not during the school year, anyway."

"I know that, too. Emma, I don't want you for a housekeeper. I want you for my wife. My granddaughters can go on cleaning for us just like they do now. Then we will have all our Saturdays to spend as we like. And Sundays. And the summer. Oh, Emma, we would be so happy together."

"That's what Mom says."

"Well, you should listen to your mother, young lady," said Aaron with a smile. "She's one smart lady. Where do you think we should have the ceremony?"

Emma looked sad at the question. "Pop says old people don't have big weddings. We would have to have it in the parlor."

"The parlor would be a perfect place. And small weddings are nice. You can enjoy your guests more that way."

"I had always dreamed of a big wedding—you know, with all the relatives and so much food that you have to cook for weeks ahead of time."

"We can have all the big gatherings we like at our own home. Let's just do what pleases your Pop and enjoy it like it was our own idea all along."

"We wouldn't be able to invite the grandchildren."

"That's fine."

"Or our friends."

"No problem."

"Or your neighbor's uncle's step-cousin on his mother's side."

"Oh, he'll be so disappointed. What was his name again?"

Emma smiled. How did he do that to her? She had just agreed to cancel her dream wedding and she was smiling. It must have been the company she was keeping.

When Emma woke on the morning of April 6, 1963, she no longer thought about the size of the wedding, nor where it was to be held, nor how much food would be served. She didn't even think of how she looked in the blue dress that she had spent so many happy hours making—well, maybe she thought about that a little.

Emma's heart was so full that morning she could think of only one thing—Aaron. She had just a few more hours to be Emma Hurst. After that, for the rest of her life, she would be Emma Hoover.

Mr. & Mrs. Aaron Hoover on their wedding day

CHAPTER 14

A New Beginning

Emma Hoover whistled snatches of *How Great Thou Art* as she circumvented the blue heating tower on the way to her car. She got in behind the wheel and threw her book bag in the backseat. Time enough for that tomorrow. Aaron was waiting.

"I'm home!" she called as she came in the back door.

Aaron snatched her up immediately and swung her around in his arms.

"How was your day?" he asked.

"It was pretty calm. Michael actually passed his spelling test. And you?"

"Oh, I'm still looking for a place for us," he said, gesturing to the bank records and real estate ads piled all over the table. "Everything is too big, or too old, or too tall, or too rickety. And they are all way overpriced. Do you know what they are asking for that place over by the creek? $32,000! And not a bit of land to go with it."

"Whew!" said Emma as she tied on an apron and set about transforming the hamburger she had thawed that morning into a quick casserole. Amazing what one could do with canned soup these days. "Maybe we should just stay here."

"Nah, the place is too big for us. I want something we can grow old in."

"Oh!" she said suddenly. "I need to get the laundry in before the dew settles. Could you watch this burger for me?"

"Sure."

Emma quickly returned with the basket of laundry and set it on the living room chair. She could fold it later. She didn't usually wash on Fridays, but they were out of towels.

"I was thinking," said Aaron, between clearing his stuff off the table, setting out the dishes, and washing down mouthfuls of casserole with large swallows of water—didn't he like her casserole?—"I was thinking we might like to try building a house."

"Really? And where would we build it?"

"Right on the corner over there." He pointed out the front window.

"Well, that would be a project. It might be kind of fun. Sawdust, plaster dust, cement under our fingernails."

"We've both done plenty of that kind of work before, even if we haven't done it all to the same building. What do you think? Should we build?"

"And you have the funds?"

"It won't cost any more than that place by the creek. And we can make things just like we like them."

Emma stared at her husband. He had that Aaron-y look about him that said, I am determined! She tried to return that Emma-ish look that said, I believe in you. And it was settled.

. . . .

"Yoo hoo! Anybody home?" Emma and Aaron looked up from the sheet of drywall they were balancing, and turned off the saw.

"John! Katie! Welcome to our new home, such as it is. Don't mind the dust."

"You two are a mess," said Katie, staring at her sister whose hair seemed to have gone white overnight.

"It's all the air pollution these days," laughed Emma as she wiped a couple of raccoon patches clear around her eyes. "Don't mind if I forgo the hugs."

"So what brings you two this way, and without the children?" asked Aaron.

"The Hurst men are looking pretty shabby," said Katie, "and they were wondering if tonight would be a good night for their haircuts. John and I were out running some errands, so we offered to deliver the message."

"They tried to phone," added John, "but I guess you were out here."

"Been working since breakfast, and I'm ready for a break," said Aaron, stretching upright and rubbing his back. "Let's head over to the old place and sit a spell."

The four of them grabbed chairs on the front porch and Emma brought out some of her famous lemonade. She always made it from the same recipe: one lemon (steeped in the water for an hour), one cup of sugar, and two quarts of water.

John took a sip and looked over at Emma. "Your lemonade is as good as ever, Emma. Do you fix it every Saturday in hopes that visitors will pop in, or do you just keep it on hand for the two of you?"

"What would you say if I told you I made it especially for you two?"

"I'd say you were lying."

Katie slapped her husband in mock defense of her sister.

"But I do have a serious question I've been meaning to ask you about," John continued. "What do you know about the rumors that the government has outlawed praying in school?"

"I don't know that they've outlawed it per se. But there have been several court cases protecting the rights of people who don't wish to be forced to pray in school."

"Isn't it the same thing?"

"Not exactly. A law is a rule that you can go to jail over. A court ruling merely sets an example for other courts to follow when they are judging cases."

"Yeah, but this was the Supreme Court."

Emma nodded. "Yes, that is more binding."

"Binding! How about un-Christian."

"Well, they are public schools after all, not churches."

"And you teach in one of those public schools. Doesn't it bother you that you can't pray anymore."

"No one said I couldn't pray, they only said it is unconstitutional to pray in a public manner. I still thank the Lord for my lunch every day."

John pursed his lips. "What good does that do the children?"

"They are free to pray too. They just can't do it in a public manner." She took another sip of lemonade.

"I can't believe you, Emma!"

Katie gave Aaron a sympathetic look. Or was it apologetic? He only shrugged his shoulders and looked at the awning.

"What's not to believe? I work for a school system in which only some of the children come from Christian homes. Would you have me go against their parents' wishes?"

"If it meant standing up for God, yes!"

"Now, John," said Katie, putting her hand on his arm. "You know Emma doesn't make the laws. She loves the Lord as much as you do."

"Care for more lemonade?" asked Aaron.

"No thank you. We just stopped to ask about the haircuts," John said. He stood up and grabbed his hat. "It's just one of those things on which Emma and I will never agree I suppose."

"Tell the men tonight would be fine." Emma said. "Seven o'clock."

"We'll do that," John said on his way down the steps. Katie gave a quiet little wave and followed close behind.

"You really shouldn't egg him on like that," said Aaron, as their company pulled out of the driveway. "You know how he feels about these things."

"He brought it up."

. . . .

Emma had trouble falling asleep that night. John's words had worked their way into her conscience. Standing up for God. What did that mean anyway? Was she supposed to make a show of prayer just so everyone would know she was a Christian? But what about the children? That was the question that really pricked at her.

She got up and turned on the reading lamp at her desk. The men's haircuts had taken up the entire evening and what with the building, doing the wash, making supper, and every other little undone thing on her list, the math papers had lain uncorrected in her bag. She set to work.

4+4=8, 6-3=3, 12+5=17…

"Trouble sleeping?" Aaron asked.

"I'm sorry, Dear. I didn't mean to wake you."

"What's the matter?"

"I've been thinking about what John said. Do you think he was right?"

"Which part?"

"That I wasn't standing up for God. And that the children might suffer for it."

"I don't know, Emma. It is a public school, like you said. Then again, isn't that why you decided to teach, so you could help the children learn how to make good decisions in life?"

"That's what's bothering me."

"Have you prayed about it?"

"Yes, but I can't seem to find an answer."

"Then come to bed and sleep on it."

"As soon as I finish this stack of papers."

CHAPTER 15

A Conflict of Interests

It was a Saturday afternoon in the summer of 1968. Emma sat in the living room holding the latest issue of the Home Messenger. Her wet hair was draped up and over the back of the chair and hung nearly to the floor.

They had been living in their new home for about a year now, and Emma felt an uncomfortable mix of gratefulness and melancholy. It was a nice enough place as far as houses go, but it wasn't really hers—at least not the way she had imagined it would be.

"This is our place as long as I'm alive," Aaron had told her, but what about after that? The house was part of Aaron's estate—part of his children's inheritance—so, if he died before she did . . .well, she just wouldn't think about it.

She composed herself as Aaron came in the front door. "Shall we have our devotions early. There's a beautiful breeze out on the porch."

the first house that Aaron & Emma built

"My hair is wet."

"Ach, just put it up in a towel and no one will know the difference."

Aaron grabbed the Bible and songbook from their place on the kitchen table and ushered Emma outside.

"You don't seem yourself tonight," Aaron said after they had finished their worship. "Something the matter?"

"I'm embarrassed even thinking it to myself; I hate the thought of confessing it to you."

"What?"

"Well, it's this house. It suits us well enough, and I really enjoyed building it with you, but if you were to go first . . . "

"If I were to go first," he finished for her, "you would be without a home."

Emma nodded. Aaron moved his chair over and put his hand on Emma's arm. "Emma, you know what it was for me to lose Lizzie. I can barely think about losing you too. But if I were to go first, you would have to suffer like I did. And the thought that you would have to leave our home too—well, I can't even think about it."

He caught her face so she couldn't look away. "What would you think about building another house? One for you. You could plan it any way you like, pick the layout, the cupboards, the fixtures. We could build it right next to this one. Then we could rent out this place and live in the new place, and whoever goes first, the other one would still have a home."

"You would be willing to build all over again?"

"Why not? We liked building this place. We'd actually know what we are doing this time."

Emma nodded.

"There's just one thing I would ask of you," Aaron said, "and it's hard for me to bring it up, because I gave you my word when I married you and I don't like to go back on my word."

"What?"

"I always kind of imagined I might retire when I turned sixty. You know, do some carpentry, a bit of landscaping, things I don't have time for now. But I would be lonely if I was by myself all day. What would you think of retiring too; then we could spend our days together building our new place? And you would have time to sew again, and to garden, and to cook."

"Don't you like my cooking?"

"Oh, yes. You're a great cook. I just think you'd enjoy having more time to do the things you like. We are getting older, you know."

Emma was silent. Give up teaching? After only ten years? "I don't know," she said at last.

"Just think about it, will you?"

Before Emma could respond a car pulled into the drive. It was Aaron's daughter Anna with her husband Lloyd and their children.

Emma loved the way Aaron's children popped in for visits. There was Anna and Lloyd, of course; Anna was the oldest. Then there was Phares with his Etta, and Mary with Paul. The next two were Elizabeth with Norman, and Alta with Samuel. And Martin with Ella Mae was the baby—if you could rightly call any thirty-year-old man a baby.

Then there were all the grandchildren; Emma's heart fairly glowed with the way they called her Granny.

"Granny! Grandpa!" squealed the younger ones as they got out of the car and ran up to their grandparents. None seemed to notice that Emma was technically a step-grandparent.

Anna greeted her father and gave Emma a big hello. She pointed to the Bible and songbook on the side table. "Did we interrupt your devotions?" she asked, trying not to notice the towel on Emma's head.

"We were finished and just about to have a little snack. Care to join us?"

Anna went in to help Emma get some cookies and lemonade ready while Grandpa and Lloyd entertained the children.

"Play us a song, Grandpa," begged little Anna Mae as she twirled a fudge-striped cookie around her finger like a diamond ring.

"A song, eh?" asked Aaron, "and what song would you like me to play?"

"One of the bouncy ones."

"All right. How about this one?" With that, he took up his mouth organ and began such a toe-tapping tune that the children bounced in their chairs. And whenever he stopped to take a breath, the smile spread so far across his face that both dimples looked deep enough that you could stick a marble in them and they wouldn't fall out. Emma liked when he looked like that.

"Play another one!" they begged when the song was finished. "No, play another two!"

"You children think I'm still in my twenties. Just one song today."

"Then Granny can tell us a story! Tell us the one about the duck and the rooster."

Emma blushed. "Oh, there are better stories than that."

"Pleeeease!"

"All right, but just once." She pulled the stool into the center of the room and looked down at the children.

"In an old farmyard there lived a rooster, a chicken, and a duck. All of them were fat and juicy-looking and they knew it. So when the preacher came to call, they hid themselves, lest the farm wife would choose one of them for the preacher's stew.

"After waiting quietly a long while, the hen peeped out." (Emma said it with a cute little peep-y sound).

"And the rooster asked" (Emma transformed her voice here to a cocka-doodle-y rooster voice), "'Did the preacher go-o-o-o-o?'

"To which the hen replied" (with a distinctly clucking voice), "'Not-yet, not-yet, not-yet!'

"The duck, worried at all the noise, finally warned the others" (in a quacking voice, of course), "'Stay BACK, stay BACK, stay BACK!'"

The adults laughed as hard as the children at Granny's barnyard sounds.

"Do it again!" the children cried.

"Once is enough," Emma said, though she was laughing as heartily as everyone else. "Let's sing a hymn instead. Do you have a suggestion, Grandpa?"

Aaron nodded. "How about, *Würdig Bist du Herr Göttlichen*?" and he led out in German.

Emma thought about the words. *Worthy art Thou Lord Divine.* Worthy of my devotion. Worthy of my adoration. Worthy of my complete surrender. Worthy art Thou Lord to receive back everything I have called my own; for it all comes from Thee.

Was God worthy enough for her to surrender her teaching career? Worthy enough that she should submit to the husband he had given her? Just how deep did her idea of God's worthiness go?

Emma knew the answer even as she sang the words. God is worthy of it all. Infinitely worthy. He would never ask more than she was able to give, but she had to be willing to surrender it all.

You are worthy, Lord. I will retire.

CHAPTER 16

No Continuing City

"Ach!" said Emma, only half out loud, as she watched the nail bag slip like a stone off the truss and fall to the cement floor below.

"You're supposed to wear that thing," said Aaron, "not perch it on the rafters like a bird."

Aaron retrieved the errant bag and climbed the ladder, only as far as was necessary to reach out and hand the bag to Emma.

"I've only got to finish this last corner and we'll be ready for the plywood," Emma said. "How are you making out with that doorway?"

"Oh, it's coming along. We will have to cut the molding a bit wider than usual to cover the gap, but no one will be the wiser."

Emma smiled with deep satisfaction. Working on this new house with Aaron was one of the most gratifying things she had ever done.

In fact, she found working on the house so enjoyable that she worried, at times, that she might be enjoying it too much.

"Now, Dear," said Aaron when she brought up the subject—again, "the Good Lord doesn't mind us enjoying our work."

"It's just that I'm so focused on it. Every day there's some new thing to get excited about: the layout, the flooring, the windows. It's all so earthly, I'm afraid it's becoming an idol," Emma said.

"You have to think about it if you're going to build it well."

"I know, but I think it consumes too much of my thought life. For example, do you suppose that God cares what kind of railings we put on the porch?"

"He cares about everything we do," said Aaron.

"I know, but does He care if they are black or white, or straight or curly?"

"I think," answered Aaron, "that He cares, but He may not have a preference, if you know what I mean. If two choices are equal, God lets us do the choosing. Of course if one choice is sinful . . ."

"I suppose. But I'm worried that I really have been letting earthly cares get hold of me. Will you pray for me?"

"Of course I will. And you can pray the same for me."

. . . .

The house was finished—or at least livable—by the spring of 1973. And what a house it was! With an attached garage and a breezeway between that was so sheltered, they could use it as a Florida room.

There were more than enough cupboards, and there was a first-floor laundry and room to lay out a quilt, and a big pic-

the second house that Aaron & Emma built

ture window where Emma could sit and watch the neighbors, or anyone else that happened to pass by. It was exactly the way Emma wanted it. It was the way Aaron wanted it too.

Well, mostly.

The one problem spot was the garage. For Aaron knew, as everybody does, that the garage is a man's place. It's the place where he can buff his car and saw his wood and leave his tools lying out wherever he wants to.

But Emma claimed, as many other people do, that the garage is a family place. It's the place where she can store last year's potatoes and press this year's cider and walk through without smudging her dress.

"Please, Aaron," Emma informed him when the house was nearly completed, "I don't want your tools scattered around that garage. I want to keep it clean."

Aaron completely understood her point of view, but it was, after all, a garage. So, when Emma was out on some errands, and the compunction overcame Aaron to organize his manly possessions, he placed his tools in and all around every available space in the garage.

When Emma saw the mess, she just cried.

It may be Emma's house, but a man needs his garage.

CHAPTER 17

The Church Sale

Emma pinned the last few garments to the line and hurried in with the basket. It was the last Saturday in July and the Martindale Church was having a sale—getting rid of old furniture and such—and she and Aaron looked forward to going.

She grabbed her purse and met him out front. He had the El Camino ready to go, figuring that, if they bought anything large, they could bring it home that day.

"Isn't it a beautiful day?" Emma said as they rode along with the windows down part way.

"Just gorgeous."

"I'm hoping they might have a nice old bench we could put in the breezeway," she said.

"I expect they might."

"Aaron, I was wondering, what do you think we should do with that border along the driveway? I was thinking some alyssums might look nice there."

"That one of those perennials?"

"No, but it's so soft and delicate, I wouldn't mind replanting it every year."

"You're the planner, Emma. Like I said, the house is yours. We built it for you. And I want you to be happy with it. If you think alyssums would be nice, we'll stop after the sale and pick some up."

"Thanks." Aaron couldn't see Emma's smile—he was concentrating too much on the road—but he heard it in her voice and it made him all warm inside.

"You enjoying your retirement?" he asked.

"You know, it's funny, but I am. I mean, I loved teaching—you know that—but being home with you is, well, freeing, if that's the right word. I never imagined I'd enjoy being a housewife, but with you as the house husband . . ."

"I told you, Emma, you're not a housewife, you're a man's wife. You're my wife."

"Yeah."

"It's been ten great years, Emma. Thanks."

"My pleasure," she said. And she meant it with all her heart.

They were almost to the church. Emma could see it on the little rise up ahead, right where the road dips down and disappears for awhile before it crests the hill.

Aaron always slowed down before he got to the top, just in case someone was coming up the other side.

As they approached the church, Aaron started to turn left into the parking lot when, suddenly, as out of nowhere, a car containing four young men shot over the crest of the hill from the other direction. It broadsided the El Camino, driving the passenger door into Emma's lap. She lost consciousness immediately.

She roused slightly. Pain! Somebody move my legs . . . No, No! . . . Not so far! My hand, my arm, it won't move. Why won't it move? She blacked out again.

Searing, inescapable agony exploded in Emma's consciousness as rescue workers pulled her mangled body from the car and lifted her into the waiting ambulance, every nerve screaming for her undivided attention. Me! Feel Me! Bone upon bone upon torn muscle and tendon. Feel me! And she was deathly cold—as if her life's energy were escaping from every exposed muscle and nerve.

Senses once used to perceive pleasure were now hot-wired for pain. The lights in the ambulance glared; the blankets crushed; the voices of the people around her thundered in her brain.

"I thought you would rush us in," said a voice from far away. It was Etta, Aaron's daughter-in-law. She was there somewhere, in the ambulance with Emma.

"I doubt we'll get there in time anyway," answered the driver. What did he mean? Emma might die before they could get to the hospital?

The ambulance banked on a curve, and Emma slammed into the mountain of blankets vainly trying to conserve her residual heat. Mercifully, she lost consciousness again.

She did make it to the emergency room, but it was a foggy, fading sort of place with more glaring lights and disembodied voices. And people. Lots of people. Etta was still beside her. So was her husband Phares—he was Aaron's oldest boy. And was that Aaron's daughter Mary over there?

Aaron! Where was Aaron? Was he all right? Before she could think of a way to voice the question, the room faded and Emma drifted into a deep, shock-induced rest.

. . . .

The first thing she noticed when she awoke several hours later was the blessed fuzziness in her brain that signaled the presence of large doses of narcotics. The second thing was the stillness of her senses.

She was lying on her back looking at the ceiling. She couldn't move her head. Something held it still. Her legs too. It was almost as if they were caught in the pincers of some giant metal crab.

Her right arm was still too. No, it was just heavy. She lifted it with great effort—just high enough to see the bulky cast wrapped clear up to her shoulder.

Her left arm seemed okay though. That was a blessing. It was about the only part that didn't hurt. But it was too busy hosting myriad mysterious tubes and wires to be of much use. She'd better let it rest awhile. She heard a nurse speaking in the room beside hers.

"Be sure to take nice deep breaths, Mr. Hoover."

Mr. Hoover! Aaron was here?

"Aaron!" she rasped, too softly for him to hear. Ach! So close, yet untouchable.

A nurse came up to Emma and explained that it was indeed her husband in the room beside hers. They were both in the ICU. She was suffering from fractures in both femurs – or thigh bones – her right knee cap, her right upper arm, her lower spine, and her twelfth right rib. She had some internal injuries as well.

The giant pincers she felt were steel splints the surgeons had clamped around her legs to keep the repaired thigh bones from shifting.

Aaron, having been on the driver's side of the car was not as badly injured. He had broken a few ribs and his cervical spine.

The nurse was reminding him, as she needed to remind Emma too, that bedfast patients with injuries like theirs must be careful to take deep breaths so fluid doesn't build up in their lungs. Otherwise they might develop pneumonia.

Emma took a few deep breaths. The last thing she needed now was to aggravate her angry wounds with fits of coughing.

Then her shoulders settled on the pillow. Aaron was okay. And she was going to be too. They would do whatever the doctors told them to so they could heal up and go home to enjoy that new house of theirs.

Too bad they couldn't be right next to each other though. That would make it so much easier.

The surgeons drilled metal pins into Emma's thighs a few days later and applied twenty pounds of pressure to each leg. With her head immobilized at the same time, she felt as if a second metal crab had joined the first, and the two were playing a monstrous game of tug-of-war with her body. The illusion was amplified by the gigantic framework the doctors had extended above and around her bed to direct the traction ropes in unthinkable directions.

Emma surrendered to the humbling routine of being fed, washed, and repositioned by other people, and she was undeterred by the pain in her ribs and abdomen when she did her breathing exercises. She was not going to get pneumonia.

Aaron did his breathing exercises too, but he did not fare as well as his wife.

Perhaps it was because he was naturally more easygoing than Emma, or perhaps it was because he was in his seventh decade of life and resting came easy. Whatever the reason, Aaron's lungs began to fill with fluid. The doctors decided to fuse the bones in his neck so he could get out of bed and move around more.

They wheeled Aaron's bed past Emma's on his way down to surgery.

"Good-bye, Emma," he said.

Good-bye? Why did he say it that way? Why not, Good morning, or, I'll see you later, or, Just a little repair job, Emma?

Emma knew exactly when they brought her husband back. Not from the sound of the gurney or the bustle of the nurses—though that would have been enough—but by his breathing. It was all wrong.

It was as if the surgeons had exchanged Aaron's lungs for those of a child and he couldn't draw in enough air to supply his fully grown body. His breaths were at the same time too shallow and too frequent, and each one sounded like he was pushing a wheelbarrow full of bricks.

"Put down your tongue, Mr. Hoover," the nurses said. But he labored on as the wheelbarrow got fuller, and the bricks heavier, until finally his breaths got too slow and too shallow for Emma to hear from her room.

Now her own heart pounded in her chest. Merciful Father, help him breathe! Please!

At about 6 p.m., exactly a week after the accident, Aaron's room went deathly still. The nurses quietly slipped off to their charts. The doctor went out and sat at the desk. Emma's Aaron, her dear sweet companion, the husband she had longed for but never dreamed she would have, passed into eternity.

Emma's soul paused. It could not process the thought. Aaron, gone? Was there such a thing? The nurses pushed her bed over to his so her left hand could touch his. It was already cool. Aaron, gone?

But . . . they'd just moved into their house. It wasn't even finished. Gone? But . . . he was only sixty-five. They had only been married ten years. And he was so healthy; it was just a fractured neck.

Emma did not cry. It was too unreal for tears. Surely her Aaron would be waiting for her when she recovered. And they would get a nice old bench or two and finish the house. And they would sit on the bench or decorate it with a basket of autumn flowers and sit out on the porch till the end of their golden years. All she had to do was wake from this nightmare.

Emma let go of the cold hand that used to be Aaron's. She would wait till the morning.

CHAPTER 18

Alone

"There you are!" said Edith, as she stepped into Emma's breezeway and found her grandmother sitting in her wheelchair before the open door, staring at the sidewalk beyond. Edith and her husband, Aaron Burkholder, had moved in with Emma to help as she recovered from her injuries. "Come, let's close this door before you catch a chill," Edith said as she reached over to grab the door handle. She stopped when she saw the tears on Emma's face.

"We were going to plant alyssum there," Emma whispered, as if talking to herself. "All along the walk. We were going to pick it up right after the sale. Aaron was going to buy it for me."

Edith stood still for a moment. Then she rested her hand on Emma's shoulder. "Alyssum would look pretty there," she said, looking out to where the crumbling brown leaves had lodged in the cracks at the edge of the walkway.

Emma stared at Edith's hand. "Aaron used to rest his hand on my shoulder like that. When I did the dishes. He wouldn't say anything; he just stood real close and put his hand on my shoulder like that. It made me feel so loved."

Edith only nodded.

"I used to wonder what it was like for him when Lizzie died. What it would be like if I lost him. But I had no idea. It's like waking up to find that the whole world is gone. And the day just goes on and on forever with no hope for the future."

"I'm so sorry. I can't begin to imagine."

"Don't try. You have your Aaron and you are both young. Enjoy him now and let the future wait."

"I'd been meaning to ask you about that. About Aaron's name. My Aaron, I mean. Does it bother you when I use his name? Would you rather I just said, my husband?"

"No. I like to hear you say his name. It seems somehow appropriate that this house should have an Aaron in it. Don't you think?" Emma gave Edith a weak and polite smile. "It's been a long day. I wouldn't mind lying down for a while."

"Sure. Let's get you settled in."

Edith wheeled Emma back to her room and helped her through the painful process of arranging her mangled body in the bed.

"Rest easy, Granny," she said as she straightened out the blanket. "Just call when you need me."

Emma waited till she heard Edith retreat to her own bedroom upstairs. Then she shifted herself on the bed, first trying to avoid her left leg, then her right arm, then her ribs. Give it up, Emma, there is no comfortable way to lie down anymore. You know that.

She finally got herself up onto her left side where she could wrap her arms around Aaron's pillow and imagine him lying beside her like he always had. Edith had changed the pillowcases often enough, but Aaron's scent still hid down in the fibers of the pillow.

Emma inhaled deeply. Aaron. Tears welled up in her eyes and her shoulders convulsed, yet she took another whiff. Then deeper. Aaron. Oh God! I miss my Aaron! She buried her sobs in his pillow and clung to it till her bones ached inside her. Oh Aaron! You said it was bad, but I had no idea how horrible!

Oh God, God, I asked You to keep my focus on spiritual things, but did I need to lose Aaron in the process? Isn't there some other way? He said this would be my house. But we meant for him to be here with me. Only four months and . . . Oh God, my focus was so temporal! I was worried about getting a bench— and about the color of the railings, and the carpet. Father, forgive me. I have been so selfish. Bring him back. Please. I cannot bear this any longer!

And so Emma mingled her prayers with her tears as she had every night since she had come home to sleep alone in their bed, until the pain was numbed by a soft sweet peace that passed all understanding. God was here with her. And He was with Aaron too. And someday, some sweet day, she would see him again.

Then she slept.

Things seemed brighter in the morning. They always did. As she did her best to help Edith clear the breakfast dishes, Emma broached the topics of grief and contentment.

"I think God has allowed all of this to come my way because He knows how badly I need to learn to be content."

"Do you think He wants us to be content with pain?"

"I think He wants us to be content with everything. Pain, joy, danger, success. It's as if life is like winding yarn onto a ball. You get some snarls here and there, then you get it straightened out and everything is going real smooth, and you feel like you have everything under control. Then suddenly the ball drops from your hands and rolls across the floor, and you have to roll it up all over again. It happens time and again, and you become frustrated and disappointed as everything tangles and you end up with more than one loose end.

"Only when we bring our life to Jesus and let Him take those loose ends and untangle those snarls, does it ever get easier. Things are never tangled for Him."

Edith nodded.

Emma continued, "I only wish I was better at surrendering my ball of yarn."

"That's a hard thing for any of us."

"So I'm learning—but on another topic." At this Emma got a decidedly Hurst twinkle in her eyes. "I've been wondering how you and Aaron fixed up your room upstairs. Would you mind if I took a look at it?"

Edith furrowed her eyebrows in a Hooverish sort of way and said, "I wouldn't mind at all your seeing it, but how would you get up there?"

"I've thought of that. You just help me get seated on the bottom step, then I can hold the railing and scoot myself up backward, one step at a time."

"I don't know, Granny. What if you fall?"

"Oh come, a girl's got to do a little living now and then."

"A little living, eh? If you say so."

Edith did her best to acquiesce to her grandmother's request, although she didn't seem to have much choice. Before Edith could think of the best way to transfer her patient from the wheelchair to the staircase, Emma grabbed her walker, hobbled over to the bottom of the stairs, and settled herself on the second step.

"There we go," said Emma as she grabbed hold of the hand rail and shifted her center of gravity. "You just stand beneath me there and I'll make my way up."

Edith faithfully manned her station as Emma pulled herself to the next step.

"So far so good."

"Does it hurt?"

"Not enough to keep me from climbing another one."

And so Emma ascended one painful step after another, like Lucy Walker making her way to the summit of the Matterhorn.

She rested at the summit, as did that heroic mountain climber, until she had mustered enough strength to rise to her feet and make her way into Edith and Aaron's bedroom.

"You've done a real nice job up here. I love the quilt."

"Thanks."

"It'll look real nice in your bedroom at home."

"If ever they get the place finished."

"Oh they will. Probably about the time I'm ready to come up here and redecorate, you'll be making your bed in your own place."

"There's time enough for that. Now how are we going to get you back downstairs?"

Emma grinned. "Same way I got up here, only in reverse." She let Edith help her down to the floor, and then descended the stairs by holding the hand rail and lowering herself to each successive step.

She took a deep breath when she reached the bottom and beamed at Edith. "That's life—made possible one step at a time."

. . . .

When, a month later, the doctor saw how rapidly Emma was improving, he gave her permission to walk unaided. Apparently he hadn't heard about her little trip up the stairs.

"Edith," she said the next day, "I think I'll go for a little walk."

Edith just stared. She had seen enough of her Granny's recovery techniques to know that discussion was useless.

"I won't be gone long. Just up and down the street."

"Okay."

With that, Emma put on her coat, wrapped her head in a scarf, and took off down the walk. What glorious freedom! No walker, no cane, nobody pushing her left when she wanted to go right.

And the sunlight. It sparkled on the snow like a million tiny diamonds. Emma smiled for the sheer beauty of it. Then she thanked the Lord that the streets were dry. As itchy as she was for a walk, she didn't think she was quite up to ice skating just yet.

She looked up at the trees, and the clouds, and the tiny drips of ice hanging from the overhead wires. What a day!

Emma walked on, lost in the pure joy of life. She hadn't felt like this since Aaron was alive. She would have skipped if she was able. Instead, she did the next best thing: she walked. And she walked. And then her legs tired, her strength waned, and she took note of where she was.

She had walked all the way to Earl Ray and Mary's house. However would she make it home?

Knowing that her enthusiasm had taken her beyond her limit, Emma trudged up Mary's driveway and rang the bell.

A surprised neighbor answered the door. "Emma!" She looked at the empty driveway. "How did you get here?"

"I stepped out for a little walk, and before I knew it, I had come farther than I had meant to."

"Well, come in. Here, I'll take your wraps. You settle into the recliner."

"Would you mind getting me a blanket for my legs?"

"Certainly. Will this afghan do?"

Emma gratefully let Mary wrap her legs in the warm blankets as she laid her head back against the cushioned rest of the recliner and sighed with satisfaction. She may have traveled a little farther than she was ready for, but it was the best walk she had ever taken.

Emma made rapid progress after that. From hobbling to driving; from squeezing therapy balls to making suits; from being spoon-fed to hosting company. And when, six months after they had come to live with her, Edith and Aaron moved into their house across the street, Emma felt ready to tackle life on her own.

But she wasn't.

She had never been alone before. First there had been the houseful of Hursts. Then there were her roommates at school and her shipmates in Europe. And then there was Aaron. Oh, Aaron. How empty the house was without him.

Emma stared at his mouth organ on the shelf and remembered the bouncy songs he had played for the grandchildren.

She couldn't help but notice the extra-wide piece of molding he had cut to cover the oversized doorway and remember the strong, manly hands that had cut it. She saw the ribbon in the Bible on the table and remembered how he had led her in worship every day of their married life.

She paced like a caged animal from window to window, searching desperately for any glimpse of another human being: someone mowing their yard, or sitting on their porch, or just driving by.

And when she saw the lights come on in all the homes around hers and imagined all the happy people behind the closed curtains, a wretched, overwhelming loneliness settled into the empty corners of her aching heart, and she wept.

CHAPTER 19

The Widows' Club

Emma patted the soil tightly down around the alyssum, wiped her hands on her apron, and sat back on her heels to examine her handiwork. Aaron would be pleased. He had been gone for three years now, and she had finally begun to move on in life. It's what he would have wanted.

Then she noticed the chickadees enjoying the sunflower seeds at the feeder she had hung in the tree on the lawn. Their little cheeps echoed the lightness in her own heart. She surprised herself by letting out a little laugh.

Emma, the widow, was laughing!

How did you do it, Lord? How did you bring joy back to my grieving heart?

I've hung onto my grief like it was my life, focusing on what used to be, or what could have been—or should have been—

if You would only have let me control events. And all along I could have been drawing strength from You. Is it just my nature to fight against loss the way I contend with You about everything else? I'm sorry, Father.

I love your little birds. They are so sweet. All they do is eat what you give them and bless others by singing grateful praises all day long. I want to be like that.

Lord, help me to be like the chickadees.

Say! Maybe I could reach out to other widows. Like Alta Nolt. She's very lonely right now. And Martha. And Lena. I could have them for a little luncheon. They don't know each other that well, but that shouldn't matter. And Dorothy would love to come too, I imagine. Let's see, that's four. Two more would be nice. Oh, how could I forget Elizabeth and Marian? They are grieving too.

Emma put away her gardening supplies and hurried in to phone the other widows in her circle of friends before some depressing thought could pounce from behind and ambush her plans.

The seven women sat in Emma's breezeway getting better acquainted between nibbles of sour-cherry danish. Sounds of contented chickadees floated in through the screened-in windows that bordered the room. The luncheon had been spectacular, and everyone was in a pleasant mood.

Emma waited for a break in the conversation to address them as a group.

"I must confess to an ulterior motive in inviting you to meet together today."

"If you're soliciting for the relief sale," said Lena, "I've already started working on a set of doilies."

Everyone laughed. Emma appreciated Lena for lightening the mood of the party.

"Actually, I have called you together for a relief project of sorts, but it is not to relieve the poor and hungry, but the bereaved and lonely. Every one of us has experienced the loss of a husband—and the loneliness that brings. And since we share a similar grief, I thought we might all be blessed by gathering to encourage one another. Something precious has been taken from us. But there is no future living in the past. We must lay aside our grief, look ahead, and go on."

"That's easier said than done," confessed one of the quieter women.

"You're right, dear," added another. "But I think Emma is right. There is a time to grieve, but it's too easy to let grief control us. There are other things in life than marriage."

"I'll confess," said another woman, "I do sometimes think that if God would just bring me someone else . . ."

"Me too," said another in a hushed voice.

"I suppose we all feel a bit like that," said Martha. "At least if our marriages were good."

"But what if God doesn't bring us someone? Should we pine away just because we are single?"

"There are worse things than being single," added Lena with a chuckle that broke the somber tone the conversation was taking.

Emma picked up on Lena's lead. "It makes me think of old Richard Martin's poor wife. That man seems to get his one satisfaction in life from making his wife miserable."

"At least she has someone to talk to," said the quiet woman. "Sometimes I'm so overcome by grief, it feels like it will swallow me alive."

"I know what you mean," said another. "When Sunday rolls around and everyone goes off to have dinner with their families, I feel like the poor skinny girl who never gets picked for the ball team. There I am, standing by the bench watching the other girls play."

"It's even worse on Sunday night," added the first. "Week after week, I sit at home alone, wondering why no one comes to visit. They came often enough when my husband was alive, but now that he's gone, it seems like they've forgotten me."

"Or when you are invited somewhere and the men come in to tell their wives when it's time to go home; I just sit there remembering when I used to have someone to come and fetch me. Now I just sit there as long as I can so I don't have to go home to an empty house."

Emma looked at the group. "I think we all feel that way at times. Let's face it, widowhood is a lonely life. But we don't have to let that loneliness conquer us. Instead, we can reach out to relieve someone else's loneliness, like we did today."

"I can't help but grieve still," said the quiet voice in the corner.

"That's okay too. You may need more time. We will all have those times when we remember and cry. But I'd like to challenge us to do all we can to let the past live in the past. God has a present for us today and a future to look forward to tomorrow."

"Even if He does not bring us another husband?" asked one of the women.

"Even if," said Emma.

And so the conversation went in and out of reminiscing, admonishing, philosophizing, and encouraging, till the afternoon turned into evening, and the women finally made their way to their single—but not quite as lonely—homes.

. . . .

Some months later, when Emma had almost forgotten the remarks she had made about how grateful she was not to have to live with a man like Richard Martin, a widower in the community began to pay her special attentions. He mowed her lawn, brought her produce, and waved when he saw her at the grocery store or along the road.

It was none other than Miserable Martin himself, who had been recently widowed, his poor wife having passed out of her suffering a few weeks before.

Oh, dear, thought Emma, as Mr. Martin's intentions became clearer with every passing wave and basket of tomatoes. God must be admonishing me for speaking unkindly of the man to the other widows.

But she also remembered what Lena had said about the situation; there are worse things than loneliness. So when Mr. Martin knocked on Emma's door to ask if he could call her on the phone from time to time, she politely informed him that she was not looking for a special friend, and thanked the Lord, once again, that he had given her such a happy—if sometimes lonely—life.

The widows met often after that, sometimes on a Sunday afternoon around one of their tables, sometimes at a restaurant during the middle of the week. And Emma found that, in reaching out to others, she had forgotten to feel sorry for herself.

a widow's club meeting

She could not imagine, though, how far God was going to ask her to reach beyond herself until she got a phone call in the spring of her sixty-second year. It was from the board of a new Mennonite school that was planning to open in Farmersville the following autumn. They wanted Emma to be the first grade teacher.

CHAPTER 20

In the Multitude of Counselors

Emma sat beside Esther at Katie's kitchen table on a Saturday afternoon in late November. Her sisters, Mary, Katie, and Alta, sat on the other side of the table. It had been several years since she had accepted the position at Farmersville Mennonite school, and the preponderance of gray hair on Emma's once-dark head gave evidence to the toll those years had taken upon her.

"So how's school coming this year?" asked Mary between bites of hard pretzel and sips of garden tea. They were Katie's staple.

"I wouldn't mind a week or two off," replied Emma, only half smiling.

"Remember how you used to wish for something to fill your lonely hours?" asked Esther.

Emma chuckled and shook her head. "There's no chance of that anymore. If I'm not directing a room full of chattering students, or explaining to their parents why they need to study their spelling lists each week, I'm correcting their worksheets till the wee hours of the morning. Oh, that reminds me, the funniest thing happened the other day. Do you know little Stefani Zimmerman?"

The other women shook their heads.

"No matter. She's one of my easier students—that is, unless we are doing an art project. It seems the girl just loves the taste of my homemade glue. She can't get enough of it. I don't know that eating it would really do her much harm, but . . .

"Anyway, the other day, when I caught her eating glue at her desk, I took the jar away and told her she would have to sit in the storeroom for a while as a punishment. She didn't complain; like I said, she is a good-natured child.

"Well, was the joke ever on me! When I was tidying up after dismissal, I noticed that the jars of extra glue I kept on the shelves in the storeroom were oddly askew. When I examined them, I found a few had been opened and there were tiny finger marks on the surface of the glue.

"Apparently my little charge had found my supplies and had helped herself to a snack during time-out."

"Ha!" Alta said as she reached into the jar for another handful of pretzels. "That's what you get for punishing the fox by giving him time-out in the hen house."

Emma chuckled. "Yes, it wasn't one of the shining moments of my teaching career." Then she sobered. "Seems I'm having a lot of teaching moments that are less than brilliant these days. I've had to go back on tranquilizers."

"Trouble sleeping again?" asked Katie.

Emma nodded. "I just don't have the stamina I once had. Not for today's children at any rate. They seem to think the world revolves around them. I spend so much time forcing them to learn the basics, there's barely time left for any of the fun activities. You know what they say about all work and no play? Well, I have a room full of dull boys."

"That bad, eh?"

"You be the judge. I have to tutor a third grade student who needs remedial work in reading, of all things. He comes from a good school system, so he's had ample opportunity to learn, but no matter how many times we review the sounds of the letters, he just doesn't seem to want to learn them."

"Maybe he has a learning disability," Katie suggested.

"Oh, I'm sure he does. But if he'd just put in a little effort, he could make some progress."

"And the others?"

"They are what you'd expect mostly. Though they have no idea what it means to study."

Katie hesitated a moment, then said, "They are very young."

"They are plenty old enough to know how to study a list of spelling words. Of course, some students are worse than others. Lamar now, he's the worst for studying. In fact, I wouldn't mind sending him home until he grows up a bit."

"What's he do that bothers you so much?" asked Mary.

"Everything's a calamity to that boy. The other day, when I insisted that he write his name on the top of his paper, he broke into such a fit of tears you would think I had paddled him with a two-by-four. Not that he wouldn't benefit from a good spanking, but the most I dare do is pull his hair as a punishment."

Mary looked sympathetic. "Did he know he was supposed to write his name on the paper?"

"Of course he did. They are required to write their names on all of their papers. He just likes to do things his own way. And when he can't, he cries.

"Take the time when he forgot to do seventeen out of sixty problems on his math test. Of course, I marked them all wrong. Well! As soon as he saw all the marked off problems, he broke into a fit of howling. I told him that if he would simply do the problems, I'd regrade the paper. And what did he do? He pushed the paper back at me and screamed that he wouldn't do it."

"Have you talked to his parents?"

"They are on the boy's side. Make up all kinds of excuses for him. Don't get me wrong, Mary. It's not that I don't like the boy. He's a dear child, and I pray constantly for wisdom on how best to handle him, but I'm about out of constructive ideas."

There was silence for a while as all the women became suddenly very interested in the ice cubes swirling around in their tea. Katie was the first to speak.

"Emma, do you think maybe it might be time for you to think about retiring? You are in your seventies."

Emma looked at her sisters. Maybe they knew her better than she knew herself. Or maybe they were just willing to face things that she refused to see.

"It has been rather difficult these last few years. What with trying to keep up with the children and still get everything else done. The school has agreed to let me off early every Friday afternoon, but I still can't seem to accomplish everything I need to do. Getting old, I guess."

Mary looked at her sympathetically. "Aren't we all."

"Maybe they could use you back at Conestoga," offered Esther. Emma had done office work at Conestoga Wood for a few years while taking a break from teaching.

"I don't know," Emma said.

"Would it help if you had an aide in the classroom?" asked Katie. "Then you could get school things done during school hours, and have time to do your house things in the evening."

"That might do it. The truth is, I'm afraid of not working. It's like Esther said, work crowds out loneliness."

"That was nearly ten years ago," said Mary. "You don't seem to be stuck in your grief anymore."

"And leaving off teaching would give you more time to do the other things you don't have time for now," said Katie.

"Like sewing men's suit coats," added Alta, with an obvious attempt to lighten the subject.

"That's the other thing," said Emma. "I'm not sure I could make it without my income. I could take up sewing again, I suppose."

"You lived on sewing income before you went back to teaching," said Mary.

"True. I will give it some serious thought. I do feel like my life is about to explode."

"Then diffuse it before it has the chance," said Katie. "Come home, Emma. Let the next generation of teachers take over. It's your turn to rest."

. . . .

"What is your opinion of the Social Security system?" Emma asked her brother Paul as they sat in her breezeway discussing retirement possibilities and watching the moon rise over the winter stars beyond the window. He had made a habit of popping in for little visits like this since Aaron had died.

"Do you mean the program in general, or whether or not Mennonites should participate in it?"

"Both."

"Well, I can't say as I see anything wrong with the program in general. Some people won't plan for their older years unless you force them to."

"And Mennonites?"

"Now that gets a little stickier. It could be considered an unequal yoke, you know. Pooling our money with the world's to make a profit probably isn't the best way of investing our savings."

"What about Christians who have already invested in the system? Is it all right for them to draw their money back out?"

"Do you want my opinion or the church's?" Paul had been ordained to the office of deacon for several years, and he sometimes had to distinguish whether Emma was asking the opinion of her little brother, Paul, or Paul, the deacon.

"Yours. I think I already know how most of the church feels."

"So you want to know what I would think about you personally tapping into the system?"

"Pretty much."

"Hmm. Yours is a particular case. The farmers now, they opted out at the beginning—most of them anyway—but in your case, well . . . that's where it gets sticky. See, in order to invest your money, they had to pool it with everyone else's. So in a sense, you became part of a gigantic, worldly corporation. Who knows where all that money has been invested all these years. Might be it was used to do some pretty harmful things."

"Farmers made money off tobacco before we knew it was harmful, and no one has asked them to refuse to draw on their savings," Emma said.

"True. Then there is the matter of receiving aid from the government. There's that unequal yoke again."

"The woman at the Social Security office assured me that the only money I would receive would be that which I myself had invested, plus any interest it has earned. How is that a handout?"

"I see your point. Like I said, yours is a rather particular case. The best I can do is recommend that you pray about it, then do what your convictions tell you to do."

"I wouldn't want even a penny that doesn't have God's blessing on it, but if it is already mine . . ."

Paul nodded his head and stared into his sister's eyes. She returned his gaze. "So you wouldn't think ill of me if I decided to draw on my account?" she asked.

"Emma, I don't think you could ever do anything that would make me think ill of you."

"You really are a help to me, you know that?"

Paul smiled. "That's what little brothers are for."

With that settled, Emma ran into the kitchen to fetch the pretzels and lemonade. It had been steeping long enough.

"So what are you going to do with all your free time once school lets out?" Paul asked as he settled himself in the chair and sipped his drink.

"Well, I've got my walk around the church in the morning—four laps makes a mile, you know."

"Does it?"

"And then there is my Bible reading."

"Yes."

"And my jigsaw puzzle. And my crypto-quiz."

"It all sounds terribly exciting."

Emma tossed a pretzel at him.

He clung protectively to his glass.

"Now, now, Emma; watch the lemonade."

"But seriously," she said, "there is plenty enough to do around here just keeping the house in order. And I thought, too, that I might make my visits to Fairmount more regularly."

"You been visiting the old folks?"

"Lydia and I were going once a week before I started at Farmersville. We would find out from the nurses who hadn't gotten any visitors in a while and go spend a little time with them."

"And you didn't find it hard thinking of things to say?"

"We often took a book along to read to them. Or we'd sing a few songs. It doesn't take much to lighten a person's day. They're so lonely there."

"I imagine."

"But they have asked me if I want to get involved with their Sharetime program where I would come in twice a month to lead an activity for the group that can't make it down to the regular activities."

"What, like doing crafts with them?"

"More like singings and group quizzes. These are the folks who can't use their hands as well anymore."

"I see. That does sound exciting, Emma. You always did like to plan things."

"I think so. And I could still keep up with my regular visits with Lydia."

"Sounds like you've got your retirement all figured out."

"Let's just say I have some plans. God has a way of changing our plans."

"Does He ever."

CHAPTER 21

Teach Us to Number Our Days

Emma stared at the rain bouncing off the porch railing and gathering in little puddles across the lawn, as an ever-widening stream of brown water tumbled along the edge of the street. As grateful as she was for the rain, she couldn't help but wonder where she was going to put everybody tomorrow.

It wasn't really her turn to host the annual Hurst reunion, but Elmer had come down with some horrible kind of skin cancer that left him hobbling on a walker. He had taken laetrile for years in hopes of staving off the dread disease that had already claimed four of his siblings, but alas...Emma couldn't begin to think of letting him and Esther host the gathering.

By all counts there would be well over two hundred people at her place tomorrow if everyone came. Imagine that many

Hursts in one place. Too bad Pop and Mom wouldn't be there too. But that generation had passed on in the last decade. Funny how the loss of her parents hadn't bothered Emma like Aaron's passing had. But they had been old, and old people die. Aaron had died before his time.

Emma kept a death registry now, listing the names of all the people she knew who had passed into eternity. She had added twenty-three names to her list in the last three months alone. It seemed eternity was creeping up on her generation too.

Now, Emma, don't go getting all teary-eyed. There's too much to do.

She pulled herself out of her sinking mood in time to catch the potatoes just as they began to boil over on the stove. See. When you dwell on the past, you mess up the present.

She tested the potatoes with a fork. Perfect. If everyone had to be stuck inside tomorrow, at least they'd all have potato salad to keep them friendly.

The next day dawned sunny and warm. The grass was still a bit spongy, but not nearly as sodden as Emma had expected.

Two hundred twenty-seven people gathered on Emma's lawn to celebrate their connection to one another, the older ones reminiscing on the wonderful times that had been, and the younger ones hoping that surely their futures would be more exciting than that.

Noah, Paul, and Ivan were practically splitting their sides as Frank recounted the time he had come hurling into the kitchen from the staircase only to land on the floor right in the middle of a group of Emma and her friends.

"Ha! That's what you get for showing off," said Noah.

"I wasn't showing off," said Frank in feigned indignation. "I was merely swinging from the molding."

"Till you lost your grip!" said Ivan, and the four brothers burst into a new round of laughter as though they had never heard the story before.

"You're one to talk," said Frank, pointing at Ivan. "Riding to the top of the silo on a rocket."

"It was an elevator," said Ivan, taking his turn at mock indignation. "And it wouldn't have gone so fast if you oxen hadn't been so big."

"Or if you hadn't been so puny," answered Frank. "We wondered if you'd ever grow up."

"Give me time," said Ivan. "I'm still working at it." At this last remark the men broke into a fresh round of laughter.

"But really, Ivan, you have come much farther than any of us expected. You're even a preacher," said Paul, "and no one expected that." Ivan had been ordained as a minister ten years before, and the two brothers shared that special kinship known only to ordained men.

"Yes, no one would have predicted that—that's for sure," said Ivan. "Say, what's the latest on Elmer?"

Paul looked sober. "Last I heard he's got tumors in his back and legs as well as on his skin. They gave him radiation and chemo, but it's not the sort of thing they can operate on."

"At least he's able to take something for the pain," said Frank.

"Yeah," said Paul.

"How's Esther taking it?" asked Noah.

Paul answered. "She's been preparing herself all these years, figuring if his brothers and sisters died of cancer, there was a pretty good chance that Elmer would come down with it sometime or other."

Ivan spoke next. "It's a good reminder to all of us to be ready. We never know when it might be our turn to meet our Creator."

A sober chorus of Amens attested to the fact that the Hurst brothers knew their days were numbered. With Mom and Pop gone, they were the elders of the clan. Only time and Providence would reveal which one of them would be next.

. . . .

A few months later, Emma's sister Mary got sick. Her arm swelled up so big she had to slit her sleeves in order to get into her dresses. Then her chest filled with fluid, and it was hard to breathe. It was breast cancer. Within a month, she was gone. Her husband, John K. Martin, was devastated.

Everyone had expected Elmer to die sometime within the next few months—his cancer was progressing so fast—but Mary? She was so healthy. So alive.

Emma got out her death registry and added Mary's name to the list.

Then Aaron's son Phares got sick. His leg swelled up like Mary's arm had. It was lymphoma, another form of cancer.

While Phares was in his first weeks of chemotherapy, Elmer passed away. On his funeral day Emma wrote in her journal: "Now there are three of us who have laid away our bosom companions, myself, John K., and Esther."

She left unspoken the question of who would be next.

She need not have asked. Four months after they buried Elmer, six months after Mary had died, while Phares was still in the middle of his struggle with that invisible enemy that stalks entire families, Katie got a headache.

It was not your everyday sort of headache, but a relentless, pervasive pain such as one would imagine radiating from a live coal buried deep inside the head.

Emma's heart broke for her sister who was convinced the family stalker had sunk its teeth into her brain and was eating her alive from the inside out.

Soon Katie was nauseated. Then tired. And her arms became too weak to hold her grand babies. John took her to the hospital for tests.

Three days later the family got the news. Katie had a golf-ball-sized tumor in the right side of her brain.

Emma went to sit with Katie at her house while John was at work. She was so glad she had retired and was free to offer Katie and John as much help as they needed.

She set her tote bag on the sofa and smiled in an effort to hide the emotions that threatened to overwhelm her. How drawn her sister looked already! And the arms of her glasses rested in her hair instead of on her ears as if the slightest pressure would feed the fire that burned inside her head. Oh God, are you taking another one of us so soon?

"You're looking good," Emma said. "How are you feeling?"

"All right, under the circumstances."

"You need anything?"

"Just company. Can you stay a while?"

"All morning. I promised John I'd fix you the best meal of left-overs you ever ate."

"Then you must have left the food out in the car because I sure haven't cooked in a while."

"John said there was plenty left from the dishes people have sent over. I'll just use that. You have much of an appetite?"

"Not much. Funny how something so basic can go away. We spend our lives watching our waistlines, worrying that we are eating too much, and then overnight it's gone."

"That is strange. I suppose God builds it into us to know when we need to eat and when we need to rest."

"I suppose so," said Katie. "You brought your handwork?" she asked, pointing to Emma's tote.

"I'm working on a baby afghan. Don't have a baby in mind to give it to, but one will come along sooner or later."

"That's for sure."

"Remember when yours were born," asked Emma, pulling a chair over near Katie's and reaching in for the baby blanket, "and I would come over to be your maid?"

"How could I forget? You were such a help to me."

"Those were great days," said Emma.

"And now they're grown with babies of their own. Mark's got his nine living, plus the one in heaven. Esther has four; David and Johnny each have seven. Can you believe the twins are going to be two come Christmas? Then Melvin and Kathryn each had five, though Kathryn lost the one. And Frank has his three. Oh, and then there are Leon's six plus two. Dear me, how could I forget? So that's how many all together? Help me think."

Emma did some quick mental calculations. "That would be forty-nine including the ones who have passed on already."

Katie smiled with deep satisfaction. "Forty-nine."

"That's a lot to be thankful for."

"I am. But you know, Emma, I used to think I'd be happy if only I could live long enough to get married. Then it was to see my children grown." Katie sighed. "But now there is this whole new batch of little ones to love, and I won't be here to see them grow up." Her lips quivered.

Emma did not know what to say. "None of it is like we imagined it would be, is it. You with almost fifty grandchildren. Me having been married, with a quiver full of step-grandchildren. Pretty good for not having had any children of my own."

That made Katie laugh. "Do you suppose you'll ever marry again?"

"At seventy-four! What kind of man would want an old hen like me?"

That made Katie laugh even harder.

"I don't know, Katie. When Aaron first passed away I thought I would die of grief. I fear I would have jumped at the first fellow who asked. But as I get older, I wonder if such a venture would be wise any more. Oh, I still have that innate longing to love and be loved, but I don't know if I could handle the drastic period of adjustment marriage brings."

"It might not be so bad now that you know what married life is like," Katie said.

"Maybe so. But I don't imagine I'll have to worry about it. Now, I'd better see to that lunch before John gets in. Even if you're not hungry, he's sure to be."

"Guaranteed."

Katie had a seizure later that day. It was but the first of many. And within a month she was bedfast, speechless, and apparently blind.

At the same time, news came in that Phares' cancer was growing again.

Katie died on July 30, 1992. Phares died eight months later.

CHAPTER 22

Of Strawberries and Fresh Asparagus

Emma braced herself on the peak of the roof, gave one last pull on the creosote brush, and shined her flashlight into the chimney. Everything looked smooth and clear. Another winter's ashes wiped away. Hard to believe it was almost a year since Katie had died.

She climbed down the ladder and stowed her tools in the garage. How Aaron would have laughed to see her hang the ladder on the garage wall. Guess he was right after all. Where else would one hang a ladder?

Emma took off her glasses and wiped the sweat from her face with the corner of her sleeve. It was unusually hot for June. Good thing she got that chimney swept out early in the forenoon. Time to head into the house to find something a little cooler to do.

As she stepped into the kitchen from the breezeway, she noticed a basket of strawberries on the table. She hadn't bought any strawberries; where could they have come from? And they looked so delicious.

Still puzzling over the mysterious berries, Emma opened the refrigerator to pull out the ice water. There, on the top shelf, right beside the water jug, was a fat bunch of tender, young asparagus shoots. What in the world? Someone seemed to have slipped into her house unawares, and graced her kitchen with the best treats from their early garden. But who? And why?

She called Esther on the phone.

"Say, would you happen to know who left some strawberries and asparagus here recently?" she asked, after the necessary preliminaries about the temperature and the amount of water in the rain gauge had been dispensed with.

"What do you mean, left some?"

"Just that. When I came in from doing my outdoor work, I found a basket of strawberries on the table and a bunch of asparagus in the refrigerator. They are obviously for me or the asparagus wouldn't be in the refrigerator."

"Someone must have slipped in while you were doing your yard work."

"No, I was up on the roof. I had a three-hundred-sixty-degree view of the area. Nobody came or left while I was up there. The best I can figure is the food was already there when I got in last night, and I didn't notice it."

"Sounds like you've got a secret pal."

"I guess so. I wonder who it is."

"If you knew, then it wouldn't be a secret anymore," Esther said with a hint of laughter in her voice. It sounded to Emma like her sister knew more than she was telling. More than likely she and John K. were behind the whole thing.

Esther with John K. Emma was still adjusting to thinking of those two as a couple. It had always been John K. and Mary; Elmer and Esther. But Mary and Elmer had died so close to each other that the widowed Hurst and her grieving brother-in-law had found themselves drawn to one another. Still, it took some getting used to.

Yes, if John K. and Esther hadn't actually left the gifts themselves, it was pretty sure they knew who did.

A few weeks later, about the time the cherries were beginning to come in, Emma got a call from John Horning, Katie's widower. He sheepishly asked Emma if she had found some . . . er, berries and the like in her fridge the other day.

John Horning? The brother-in-law who was personally offended that Emma hadn't objected to the removal of prayer from the schools? The John with eight children and six times as many grandchildren? Katie's John? Why, he and Emma were as incompatible as an oak and a tornado. If he had left the gifts, it must have been out of a sense of compassion or duty.

Then why did he give the gifts anonymously? And why did he wait three weeks to own up to the deed? Emma's stomach felt strangely a-flutter.

Esther phoned her back a few days later. "John K. and I have been wanting to make a trip up to Longwood Gardens for a day. We were thinking that, as you and John Horning don't get to do things like this anymore, you both might like to come along. So John K. called John Horning and asked him about it, and he liked the idea. What do you think?"

Emma paused before responding. "Would it be just the four of us?"

"Well, yes. We could all fit in one car that way."

Emma's stomach started to flutter again. "Did John know you'd be asking me along before he said yes?"

"He sure did. Matter of fact, John K. says that John Horning liked the idea of a foursome."

"Did he now?" Emma wondered if her sister could hear her smiling through the phone lines. "I've wanted for a long time to visit the gardens. When were you thinking of going?"

"Friday a week."

Emma's shoulders drooped. "That's the day I promised a friend to go to Indiana with her. I guess you three will have to go without me."

It was Esther's turn to be silent. "Let me talk to John K. and see what he thinks about fixing on another day."

"How would the 10th suit?" Esther asked over the phone a few days later. "John Horning has the day free, and it's a Tuesday, so we'll get a seniors' discount."

"Oh, Lord," Emma prayed when she got off the phone. "I feel like a school girl. To think, someone might be interested in me. Then again, perhaps you are just testing me. I don't want to run ahead of your will, Father, but maybe my caution is just my schlosslich nature holding me back. How can I know? Oh, Father, see me through this time and have your own way with me. Thy will be done, oh Lord. Thy will be done."

. . . .

A few sleepless nights, and as many stomach-fluttering days later, Emma found herself perched on the edge of the reflecting pool at Longwood Gardens. John really had wanted to spend the day with her; it was not just a test.

She looked at herself in the pool: a few wrinkles, slightly crooked smile, radiant. John's face smiled up from beside hers: thinning gray hair, beaming smile, playful. He dropped a penny into the glassy pool and grinned as their combined reflections morphed into an undulating circle of sparkling waves.

"Let's walk around the lake," he said as he helped Emma up and led the way down the path.

"You should come to live with me at Brickerville," he said, as they rounded the northern edge of the lake.

"Aren't you getting ahead of yourself, Mr. Horning?" Emma asked.

"Ahead of myself? I announced my intentions several weeks ago."

"When?"

"When I brought you the berries," he said with a shy grin.

"The berries!" she replied.

"Yes. The berries. And if that didn't tell you what I think of you, the asparagus surely did."

Emma giggled. "I've heard of a lot of romantic ways to pro- pose to a girl, but anonymously leaving asparagus in her fridge is the most creative one yet."

"Didn't you like the asparagus?"

"Immensely."

"See then; it was the perfect way to propose."

"John, you are as incorrigible as ever. And if I did marry you, it wouldn't be to move to Brickerville; my house is a whole lot nicer."

"Then I'll come live with you," he said.

"I do have to admit," Emma said softly, "since I found out it was you who left the food in my kitchen, I have kind of hoped they were more than just the overflow from your garden."

"And now that you know?" he asked, stopping and looking Emma straight in the eyes.

"Now that I know, I can hardly believe it. After I lost Aaron, I thought my world had ended. Then when I was finally able to get over my grief and look forward in life, I found I had become an old woman. Too old to teach any more. Too old to switch careers. Certainly too old to ever again be attractive to a man."

"You're wrong there, Emma. You have so much life in you. So much bubbly joy. I need that in my life. I was like you, thinking the world ended when Katie died. But when I looked up, there you were, almost waiting for me—not that I thought those things when Katie was around."

"No, of course not. But we've been sister and brother-in-law all these years. It's hard to imagine our relationship being any different."

"John K. and Esther seem happy enough," said John, as he led Emma around the lake and into Pierce's forest.

"When Aaron and I got married," said Emma, "he found it hard sometimes to adjust to the ways in which I was different from his first wife. It would be twice as hard for us, I imagine— with you expecting me to act like Katie and me expecting you to react like Aaron."

"Oh, I don't know as it would be like that. We've known each other since our twenties."

"And when you wake up in the morning and see me with my hair all matted up and bags under my eyes?"

"I'll give you a big toothless grin and tell you you're the prettiest girl I ever laid eyes on." A smirk spread its way across his face as he added, "Then I'll put my glasses on."

Emma gave her purse a playful swing in John's direction, then reigned it in when she heard Esther and John K. on the path ahead of them.

"Look at these azaleas!" exclaimed Esther. "I didn't know they came in red."

Emma surveyed her surroundings and realized they were in a wooded area. There were flaming red azaleas all along the path on which she and John had been strolling. When had they left the water garden?

"You two hungry at all?" asked John K. "There is a nice restaurant in the Terrace building by the conservatory. I hear they have good food."

Emma looked at her companion for direction. Somehow, between the time they had entered Longwood Gardens as brother- and sister-in-law, and the time they had found themselves on the azalea path, John and Emma had become a couple. And somewhere between the path and the time John clasped Emma's hand on the drive home, they became engaged.

. . . .

John called or visited Emma every day that week, even brought his tape measure along one day so he could measure her garage door.

"Plenty of room," he told her as he retracted the tape.

Emma raised her eyebrows. "That's terribly romantic of you, John."

"Well, I have to have a place to park my truck."

"And if your truck is too small for my garage?"

"Then I'd let you buy me a new truck." John winked at Emma.

She smiled in return. "You're as hopeless as ever, Mr. Horning."

CHAPTER 23

Second Honeymoon

Emma looked up as John pulled into the driveway in a big truck with the logo, Paul B—Hardware blazoned across the side. Though they had been married over a year, Emma still got excited when John ran deliveries for Paul B's, because that meant he got to come home for lunch.

"Got another one?" John asked, as he stepped into the breezeway and saw Emma counting the spent shotgun shells she had collected on the windowsill. There was one for every sparrow who had ever had the misfortune of coming under her aim.

"Three, actually. You should have seen how they were bullying my chickadees."

"So what's your count up to?"

"Thirty-seven here in the breezeway and I don't know how many in the bedroom."

"All I can say is I'm glad you keep the casings and not the birds."

"Hey. I'm a pretty good shot, and you know it. Why, just today I hit a porch railing."

"You what? Who's porch railing?"

"Harvey and Rhoda's."

"Do they know yet?" asked John.

"Rhoda came over soon after the shot went wild. She said she was in the house when she heard a ding on the porch. When she came out to see what had made the noise, she found my pellets."

"It's a good thing you didn't hit one of the grandchildren. Did you save the shell?"

"Of course," she said, holding up an empty cartridge and beaming with pride. "But speaking of grandchildren, when I went to divide up the candy for them this morning, I found I didn't have enough bags. Would you mind bringing some home tonight?"

"Why don't you ride along with me? I've got some deliveries to make in the south end of the county, and we could stop for bags while we're out."

"The laundry's not hung yet. And I haven't even started lunch."

"Just fry up some scrapple; I'll hang the laundry."

"It's just the whites there," she said, pointing to the basket of wet laundry on the chair. Just hang it on the rack."

With that, Emma went into the kitchen to throw together a meal. Her stomach turned at the thought of the fried meat. Maybe the pudding that was setting up in the fridge and a warmed up jar of potato soup would make it more palatable. Emma winced as she unwrapped the prepared loaf and cut a few slices, a thick one for John and a sliver for herself. She normally liked the loafed meat, but today she just wasn't hungry.

She threw the meat slices into the pan and recoiled. Ugh! The smell! And the hot grease; it was almost too much. She curled up her lip and turned on the overhead fan.

"You're not eating much these days, Dear," John said when he observed the tiny portions on his wife's plate. "Are you on a diet?"

"Just not hungry."

"Well, this pudding's delicious. What are the little chewy bits; coconut?"

Emma laughed. "That and a hundred other things. I started out with a recipe, but it seemed too runny, so I threw in a bit of clear gel to thicken it. But that made it too lumpy, so I ran it through the blender which made it runny again. So I added some potato flakes, and a bit of coconut, and a spoonful or two of tapioca, and there you have it; never to be duplicated."

"Too bad. This would definitely have been a favorite."

. . . .

"Where would you like to stop for those candy bags," John asked later that day as they were driving up from New Holland after their last delivery.

"I think I'll just skip it for today," Emma said in a voice that was strangely quiet. "I'll get them with my regular groceries on Friday."

John glanced away from the road to take a quick look at Emma. "Something wrong?"

"Just a little tired. This old body isn't what it used to be."

"Did you get your nap this morning?"

"Two of them," Emma said. "The first one right after you left for work and another around ten o'clock."

"Maybe you should see the doctor."

"We'll see."

Emma skipped church the next few Sundays. She was just too tired to go. Then she developed a low-grade fever. And she lost weight. She slogged through the spring, getting weaker and increasingly sluggish with each passing day. By the time the potatoes were ready to dig in July, she was downright lethargic.

"I'm sorry, Dear," she said to John as she unslung the bag from her shoulder and let it fall to the ground after gathering only a dozen or so potatoes. "I'm just so tired. I think I'll go in and lay down a bit. Would you mind bringing in my bag?"

She dragged herself to the house, using the hoe as a prop. Her husband looked on with worried eyes.

He took her to the doctor the next day. They said she had a virus. A few days later, they said she had heat exhaustion. Then they said she had shingles. By the middle of August, when the buttercups were growing wild around Mary's and Katie's graves, they said that which she had suspected all along. Emma had cancer.

It was not the fast-growing breast cancer that had destroyed Mary's lymphatic system in little more than a month, nor was it the burning tumor that ate away at Katie's living brain. Emma's was a slower moving, stealthier stalker; she had cancer of the bladder.

She had seen the blood in her urine, felt the strange fullness in her abdomen, been overcome by the inexplicable need to rest. When the urologist told her she would need both surgery and chemotherapy, Emma agreed without argument; if it was the end, at least she would get to rest. She wrote in her journal:

"Life's evening sun is sinking low, a few more days and I must go, to meet the deeds that I have done, where there will be no setting sun . . . Lord, remember me!"

The surgery was not a big deal—just a scraping of the tumors from the inside of the bladder in the day-surgery unit—but the weeks of chemotherapy were more exhausting than the cancer itself. John's granddaughter, Sylvia, Mark and Lucille's daughter, came to help Emma when John was at work.

"Now where are you headed?" Sylvia asked as Emma dragged herself to the kitchen to get the window cleaner and a rag.

"This picture window is covered with spots," she said, pointing to the large window in the living room, "and they are driving me to distraction."

"Oh, no, you don't," Sylvia said as she helped Emma settle into the recliner. "You're supposed to rest. You just sit back in that chair and I'll do the windows. Here's today's paper. You haven't done your puzzle yet."

Emma took the paper and smiled lovingly at her adopted granddaughter. "You are such a jewel. I don't think I could manage without you."

"If it wasn't me, then Aunt Grace or Rhoda or one of the other granddaughters would be here."

"Yes," said Emma, "but you're here today, and I thank you."

CHAPTER 24

A New Millennium

Emma set her bread dough aside to rise and turned her attention to cleaning out John's lunchbox. She dumped the orange peels from the box into the garbage disposal and flipped the switch. There was a horrible crunching sound as the machine ground up the peels. Must have been some particularly hard pits.

It had been five years since her diagnosis of cancer, and though she was a bit drained from the repeated scrapings needed to keep her bladder free from tumors, she could manage her tasks without too much help from the grandchildren.

She washed out the Thermos bottle with hot sudsy water and set it in the drainer to dry. Then she headed out to the breezeway to join John for their evening devotions.

"I've been thinking I might retire from driving the deliveries," John said as Emma sat down in the chair opposite his.

"I thought you liked driving the truck," she said.

"I do. But I liked it better when you came along."

"Doctor Teodora says I'm to take it easy."

"I know. I just miss you."

Emma smiled at her husband. "I miss you too." After a slight pause, she added, "Will you leave Paul B's altogether?"

"No, they've been teaching me how to run that computer cash register they have up front, and I'm actually getting the knack of it."

"My John on a computer? Who could have imagined."

John runs the computerized cash register at Paul B's

"Hey!" he said, "this is the year 2,000; we're in a new millennium."

"I believe 2,000 is the final year of the old millennium," Emma said. "The new millennium doesn't technically start till next year."

"Technicalities. Who cares about technicalities?"

"You'd better, if you're going to run a cash register."

"All I do is punch a few buttons and it does all the figuring. Wish they'd had machines like that when we were in school."

"Then you would have forgotten how to count." Emma grinned. "Speaking of forgetting, did you remember to get a new battery for your hearing aid?"

"Now look who's forgetting. Don't you remember I picked one up at Royer's last Friday?"

"Ha! You got me there. Is the world sounding any better?"

"A bit, but I had to take it out at lunchtime."

"Lunchtime?" Emma asked, as a dreadful thought arose in the back of her mind.

"Yeah, it was rubbing terrible on that sore spot."

"Where did you lay it when you took it out?"

John looked toward the ceiling as he searched his memory. "In my lunchbox."

Emma's jaw dropped as she looked at him with dismay. "Where in your lunchbox?"

"Next to the thermos. By the cap."

"I washed the thermos and there was nothing there." She jumped up and ran to the kitchen. John got up as quickly as his aging knees would allow and followed her.

Emma frantically searched through the lunchbox, the thermos, and the area around the sink. She even pushed the rubber flaps back around the mouth of the disposal unit and peered into the cavity. Then she began to cry. There they were, tiny shreds of pink plastic lodged between the blades. The remains of John's hearing aid.

"Oh no!" she said, turning to look at John. "What a dunce I am! I put your hearing aid through the garbage disposal."

John put his arm around Emma. "That's okay. It wasn't work-ing very well anyway."

"I feel like such an idiot."

"Don't even think about it. It's just God's way of getting me to do what I've been needing to do for months. You know I've been thinking about getting a Miracle Ear. And you're starting to need one yourself. We'll just call and make an appointment for both of us."

"Miracle Ears are expensive. Two would be outrageous."

"That's for me to worry about. Come on, it's time to sing; I'll clean out the disposal later."

. . . .

Four years passed, and Emma came to appreciate her new hearing aid. Mostly. While it made the preacher's words crisper, and she could once again pick out the lower tones of her beloved songbirds, the device also magnified obnoxious noises—like the annoying chirp emanating from the toy John was playing with in the living room.

"Isn't that for the grandchildren?" she barked.

"Cute, isn't it?"

Apparently John had missed the tone in her voice. As if it weren't enough that he sat there playing with a child's toy while she struggled to swing the ridiculously heavy mop across the kitchen floor, she had to listen to him pull the string over, and over, and over again.

Chirp, chirp, chirrrrrp… it went again.

"Did you hear it long enough yet!?" she growled. There was no way he could mistake her tone this time.

He looked up. "Is something wrong?"

"Just me trying to lift a mop-head the size of a backhoe while that toy keeps making that obnoxious sound."

John put down the toy and took the mop from Emma's hands. "Whoa, is this the mop I got you from Paul B's?"

Emma nodded.

"It's the industrial model for sure. Did you wring it out well?"

She gave him a look that as much as said, What do you think! "The handle is almost too heavy by itself, but the mop-head holds so much water I can hardly lift it, let alone swing it around."

"Here, let me finish the floor," John said. "Then you can finish the rolls."

"Thanks. I'm sorry I snipped at you."

"Does that mean I can play with the toy again?"

Emma would have swung the mop at him… if only she could have.

"We're slowing down, Mr. Horning," she said as she plucked off chunks of dough and formed them into little balls. "You with your knees, and me with my cancer."

"At least we can still get around," he said. "That's more than a lot of folks our age can say."

"You give any more thought to buying a scooter?" she asked.

"Oh, I don't think I'm to that point quite yet. Let's see if a knee replacement won't do the trick. If it doesn't, well, then we can think about a scooter."

"Are you still glad you married me?" Emma asked, as John washed the floor.

John looked up, startled. "Why? You're not sorry you married me, are you?"

Now Emma looked startled. "Oh, no. I was just thinking what a burden I've been to you. In and out of the hospital for scrapings all the time. Can't swing my own mop."

"Emma, you're the best thing that ever happened to me. And I don't mind taking you to the doctors. I just wish you didn't have to suffer so much. I'd fix it if I could."

"So you don't think it was a mistake for us to marry in our sunset years."

"They'd have been dismal years if we had stayed apart, so let's just thank the Lord for bringing us together. Besides, it's like I tell John K., We were lucky enough to get Hurst girls in the first place. We're twice as lucky to be able to come back for seconds."

. . . .

Emma hummed as she took the rolls out of the oven a few hours later. The floor sparkled. Leave it to John to do it just the way she liked it. And tomorrow was Sunday—the best of days— and she would get to enjoy it with John. What a blessed woman!

She went in to get washed up and ready for bed. It was then that she noticed she had clots of blood in her urine.

CHAPTER 25

A Body to Surrender

"The tissue is too scarred," said Dr. Teodora as she sat down on the rolling stool and tucked her long brown hair behind her right ear. "We've scraped your bladder thirteen times, and there is nothing left to work with. We have no choice this time but to remove the entire bladder."

"And wear a bag," said Emma.

"And wear a bag," echoed the doctor. "We would build a new bladder from a section of your intestine, but it would need to empty into a pouch attached to your abdomen."

"That's major surgery."

"Very major."

"And I can't have any more chemo?"

"That's right."

"What if I choose to do nothing?" Emma asked.

"Then you will be choosing to let the cancer take over." Dr. Teodora paused a moment, then continued. "I'm not trying to pressure you, Mrs. Horning. I just need to make sure you understand all the facts. The choice of whether or not to have the cystectomy is completely up to you. Why don't you take a few days to consider it, then call me with your decision. Just don't take too long."

. . . .

Sylvia stopped in the next day to see how Emma was getting along. "You look tired, Granny," she said, as she sat down across from her intermittent patient in the living room. It was a particularly cold day, even for February, and Emma was enjoying the cozy warmth of the wood stove.

"I'm exhausted," said Emma. "I took a sleeping pill last night and all it did was leave me feeling groggy when I woke up."

Sylvia nodded. "Sometimes it's more restful to lay awake a few hours and let sleep find you naturally."

"I tried that, but I couldn't shut my brain down. It's this cancer."

"What did the doctor say?"

"She says my bladder is too scarred to take any more scrapings. I know she's right; I saw it on the video of my cystoscope. I don't know, Sylvia; I'm eight-five. Do you think a woman my age should subject herself to something as major as a cystectomy?"

"You're a pretty healthy woman. I think you could handle the surgery. What does Grandpa say?"

"He'll support me either way, but I know he wants me to go ahead with it. It's too much like Katie all over again, and he's afraid of losing another wife."

"I can certainly understand that."

"What troubles me," said Emma, "or at least keeps me from falling asleep, is trying to figure out what God's will is in all this. He's certainly capable of healing me miraculously—I know that better than anyone—but He also uses doctors. So I'm torn; should I submit my body to the surgery or be content with the way things are now? God might be chastising me just to remind me of how frail I am. Which reminds me," she said, reaching over and grabbing a book from the table beside her, "I came across this when I was looking for something to focus my thoughts last night, and I thought you might like to borrow it."

Sylvia took the book and looked at the cover. *The Christian's Secret of a Happy Life*, she read aloud.

"I found that on your great-great grand-pap's bookshelf years ago. It reminds us that we can trust God to take care of us, even when circumstances seem their darkest. It's life-changing."

"Thanks, Granny."

"Take care you don't get anything on it; it's the original copy."

"I'll treat it like my own."

. . . .

Emma poured a bit of water over each of her amaryllis plants. What a glorious display they made on the windowsill! The red one was her favorite, probably because it was given to her by her sister Alta, who loved the brilliant blooms as much as Emma did.

It had been weeks since Dr. Teodora had told her to make her decision. Weeks in which the cancer might have escaped her bladder to steal, unnoticed, through her bloodstream to every organ of her body. The thought made her shudder. It wasn't faith that made Emma waver; it was fear. And she knew it.

She called the doctor's office and told them she was ready to have the surgery. They had an opening April 17th. Then she called Paul to schedule an anointing service. The least she could do was give God one more chance to do things His way. Then if He didn't heal her miraculously, she'd know it would be okay to let Him work through the surgeons.

Thirty-five people came to the anointing service, most of them Hornings, though Paul and Frank were there as well. "God brought all these ups and downs on me to keep me humble," Emma said, after the bishop had poured the oil on her head and prayed for the Great Physician to reach down and heal her diseased body. And though she was as sure of God's love as she was of her own name, Emma still had misgivings about the surgery.

On April 16, the day before her bladder was to be removed, she visited Dr. Teodora in her office.

"I have changed my mind," Emma said to the doctor. "I've decided not to subject my whole body to such a drastic surgery."

"You realize the cancer is likely to spread if you do nothing," the doctor said.

"I realize that. But I've decided to let God deal with my problem His way."

"Have you considered that His way may include the use of surgery?"

"I have. But I must trust Him beyond everything else. If it is His will that the cancer spreads, then that is my will too."

"That is certainly your decision to make. We will be here whichever way you decide. If you don't have the surgery and the cancer does spread, we will do all we can to make things as comfortable for you as we can."

"I appreciate that," she said as she rose and stepped toward the door. "You have been a great blessing to me, Doctor. I will never forget all you have done for me."

Paul applauded her decision. John wasn't so sure.

. . . .

April passed. Then May. As the pounds slipped off her already-wasted body, Emma wondered if she had thrown away the last chance God was going to offer her.

"Are you sure you've made the right decision?" John asked, as he watched her bubbly spirit slip away with each diminishing pound.

"How can I know?" she said with tears in her eyes. "How can anyone know the will of an unknowable God?"

"He's not unknowable, Emma."

"He's beyond my comprehension. What do you think He wants me to do?"

"Truthfully?" John asked.

"Truthfully."

"I think He's blessed you with a mind that can think and a doctor who knows what's best for you."

"So you think He wants me to go ahead with the surgery?"

"I do. I've watched you toss and turn and fret over this decision for half a year and it's obvious you're not at peace."

"And you don't think having the surgery would indicate a lack of faith?"

"It takes as much faith to let a surgeon cut you open and remove part of your insides as it does to sit back and wait for a miracle."

"Paul wouldn't agree with you."

"Maybe you don't know his mind as well as you think you do."

"Oh, John. It's all so confusing. I wish I didn't have to choose. Would that God would just reach out and make the choice for me."

"That's what He gave you a brain for, Emma."

"But this is such a huge decision."

"So are a lot of things in life."

. . . .

Emma called Dr. Teodora's office the next day and apologized for having been so indecisive—and so stubborn. When she asked if she had delayed surgery too long, the doctor told her there was still hope that the cancer hadn't spread, and she scheduled a CT scan for July 8.

Poor Emma. She was so distraught by this time that she showed up at the x-ray department on the 9th, a full day late. The soonest they could reschedule her would be the 20th, and the soonest she could see Dr. Teodora after that would be the 29th; that was three weeks away!

Emma went out to her car and wept. What a fool she had been. She had waited too long. And now God was allowing her to receive the recompense for her own stubborn will. "Oh Father," she cried, "I'm so sorry. So wretchedly sorry. Have mercy on me and forgive my stubborn pride. I really do want your will, oh God. And if this be it, then help me to be content."

. . . .

"Your bladder and surrounding organs look good," the doctor said when they finally met in her office three weeks later."

"So there is still a chance for the surgery."

"Definitely. In fact, since it doesn't look like an emergency at this point, I think we can put you on the normal surgery lineup. You think you can clear your calendar by the first week in September?"

Emma smiled. She was so worn down, she wasn't even canning this year. "Yes, I think that could be arranged."

When Emma got home, she found she had a lot more things to arrange than she had imagined. There were meals to make and freeze for John to eat when she was recuperating; there was the bedding to do and hang out one last time before the days turned colder; there was the quilt top to finish, and the garage to clean out, and the amaryllises to get out of the basement.

Oh, the amaryllises! John wouldn't remember to water them. Would they survive till she got back on her feet again? If she got back on her feet again.

Stop that, Emma. Just give the bulbs to Alta. She'd love to add them to her collection.

. . . .

September came before Emma was ready to face it. Not that one is ever really able to face the thought of having their body cut open and their vital organs ripped out and cast aside.

Thankfully, she was unconscious throughout the entire surgery, and when she woke, she felt as complete a person as she had been when she had entered the operating room. More than complete really, for she now had one additional body part, a urostomy bag that, when not leaking, held the urine she had hitherto stored in the less visible parts of her anatomy.

CHAPTER 26

A Will to Surrender

"To think of all the pain and hassle I put up with having those scrapings every few months—not to mention the cost," Emma said to John as she adjusted her dress more discretely over her urostomy bag. "If I'd have known what little fuss this bag really is, I think I'd have taken Dr. Teodora's advice years ago."

"You know what they say about hindsight."

"Yes, well it seems I'm a slow learner. I think I'm ready now."

The two of them headed out to do a bit of work around the yard. John had retired nearly two years ago—just a few months after Emma's surgery—and they did a lot of the chores together now. It was a good thing too for, between his worsening arthritis and her altered urinary system, it took both of them twice as long to do what either of them alone used to accomplish in half the time.

"Oh look!" cried Emma as she bent over to pick up the bird feeder that lay smashed on the ground beside the wall of the house. It was one she had built a few years ago so she could watch the birds up close to the house. "I worried about this when I heard those winds last night. It blows terribly along this side of the house."

"Why not hang it on the clothes pole?" asked John.

"I want to be able to see the birds from the window. Plus, I'm afraid if I move the feeder, it might take the birds awhile to find it again. They've come to expect me to feed them."

"It's summer; they won't starve," John said, the voice of practicality in an otherwise emotional situation.

"I guess I could put it over in the tree," Emma said, gesturing to the maple across the walkway. It was big and ivy-covered and offered a substantial shelter from the wind, especially on the lea side.

"What about the squirrels?" asked Mr. Practicality.

"Just let them try to bother my birds, and I'll shoot them before they can say sunflower seed."

John grinned. "Glad I'm not a squirrel."

Emma gathered the bent and twisted segments of the feeder that had brought her so much joy during her months of healing and carried them into the garage. She set them on the workbench and got out her tools—hammer, pliers, nails. The wood was still good, just disassembled. All she really had to do was pull out a few twisted nails and replace them with new ones. It didn't take long.

She took the feeder over to the tree. The ivy on it was rather thick; she had to work it aside so she didn't harm it as she nailed the feeder to the trunk and added a few braces for extra strength. There. That ought to do it.

Now for the birdseed. She dumped a small pile of black-oil sunflower seeds into the hopper, then set up a lawn chair in the garage—just far enough in the shadow of the doorway so as not to be visible to the birds. She sat down to wait.

Wait? For what? Emma had no sooner adjusted her dress around the scratchy fibers of the lawn chair than two birds settled on the feeder and began to eat. Three more perched in the branches of the tree in a sort of holding pattern. Isn't that something, she thought. They must have been watching me the whole time.

She marveled at the way the tiny creatures took to their new location. It was almost as if they didn't notice the change at all. If only she could be as adaptable. For months Emma had resisted the only treatment that would really make any long-term difference in her health, and she had suffered needlessly as a consequence. I don't want to have surgery, she had reasoned. It costs too much. I'm too old. And on and on. Seems the birds are wiser than me in a lot of ways.

Isn't that the biggest battle after all, to be meek, to let God say when and where we are going to feed, and even to choose the style of seeds we will get?

Perhaps birds understand something about their Creator we humans have trouble getting hold of. Or maybe it's just that they understand how tiny they are in His scheme of things.

"Emma!" John yelled from the back yard. "Can you come help me with this mower?"

She hurried around the house to find her husband struggling to pull out the oil filter with his right hand while he balanced on a cane with his left. His back and knees had been giving him so much trouble lately that he had become rather prone to falling.

"The thing keeps quitting on me. I think all it needs is a new filter, but I can't get a grip on the old one."

"Here, let me see," she said as she wrapped her small fingers around the filter and removed it in one smooth pull. She saw the discouraged look on her husband's face as she did so. "You must have really loosened that thing before I got here. It was practically out."

Truth was, John's fingers were succumbing to the same crippling arthritis that was sabotaging the use of his legs. Emma felt bad when she had to help him like this; she knew he felt robbed of his manliness as well.

John helps Emma fix the windmill

"I think I'll stay home from the sale tomorrow," John said, as he climbed onto the mower and settled himself behind the steering wheel. "You can go on with Mark and Lucille." The relief sale was that time of year when everyone, regardless of whether they had made anything to sell, gathered to raise money for the poor. John and Emma had gone every year.

"I don't want to go without you."

"You'll have fun."

"Not without you."

"If you wait for these old joints to be up to walking around the sale yard again, I'm afraid you'll be waiting forever."

"You can bring your walker."

"Then my arms will tire out. No, Dear. You go with Mark's, and I'll rest up for Sunday."

Emma finally agreed to go, but her heart wasn't in it. Not without John.

A few weeks later John borrowed a motorized Pronto scooter from Harvey Weaver. It seemed Harvey kept it around just so he'd have it to lend out to folks who needed it.

Emma got out her carpentry tools again.

"What are you doing in the garage?" asked John, when she came in to measure the doorway.

"Building a ramp. I want to be sure it's wide enough."

"For the Pronto?"

"Mm-hm."

She had built two houses with Aaron. Surely she could build a little ramp for John. Well, relatively speaking. For, little as the ramp looked when placed beside a house, it was almost too heavy for her to maneuver into place. But she was Emma, after all, and she had made up her mind.

"There," she said, as she stood up to survey her handiwork. The ramp fit snugly against the doorway, a perfect fit. "Now you will be able to come and go as you please."

John nodded.

"Speaking of which," she continued, "what would you think about heading over to Fairmount tomorrow to catch the afternoon services? Glen Wise is preaching, I hear."

"I don't think the scooter would fit in the trunk," John said with a playful smirk.

Emma caught his look and grinned like the Cheshire cat. "No silly, I was thinking you could ride it all the way to the Home."

"With you on my lap?"

"No, I'll stand on back like a dogsled driver and crack the whip if you go too slow through the intersections."

"Ah, you're good for me, Emma. No, I think I'll just take my walker. That is, if you don't wear me out today."

"No sir," Emma said with a satisfied smirk of her own. "Today you shall sit around and eat cookies."

. . . .

Emma dropped John off at the front door of the assisted living center at Fairmount Home, and then parked the car. She met him in the lobby, and they walked into the chapel together.

The chapel at Fairmount was a good-sized room, with blue carpeting, four rows of convention hall chairs, and a peak in the ceiling that made the place feel somehow churchier than the other rooms in the building. A row of chairs lining the wall beyond the pulpit completed the mood.

Emma sat in the second seat from the aisle. John took the end, partly because he felt more like he was adjoining an imaginary men's side, and partly because he needed a place to set his walker.

The room was filled with a variety of styles and subcultures, though most of them were Mennonites of one form or another: residents, visitors, conservative, liberal, old order, Amish, and everything in between.

"A wise man is strong, yea a man of knowledge increaseth strength," said Glen Wise, repeating a portion of the text that had been read minutes before by Elvin Martin. It was a verse that Emma knew well.

She looked around the room. There were plenty of wise people there, but strong? Not if you judged by their rubber-tipped walkers and withered legs. But Emma knew the psalm was referring to a different type of strength. It was a strength of the soul.

She looked at John, his walker folded beside him like a dozen other wizened people in the room. Her heart cried inside.

They visited a number of old friends after the service, many of them in tiny rooms in the assisted living wing, a few in the complete care center.

"Do you think we'll ever end up here?" John asked as they made their way down the hall toward the lobby.

"Oh, I don't know," Emma said. "Not for a long time anyway."

John paused to stare into one of the bedrooms as they passed. "I'm not sure, Emma. The time comes for all of us."

CHAPTER 27

I Surrender All

Emma hung her broom on the garage wall and massaged her right hip. It had been aching lately.

It was the summer of 2007, the thirty-fifth year she had cleaned out this garage and put it back in order. The floor wasn't as nice as when she used to scrub it on her hands and knees, but it looked pretty good anyway. It ought to; she had worked all morning. She went into the house to wash up and fix lunch.

She found John at the kitchen table with his file cabinet. His ledger and calculator were open, and some other papers were spread across the table. Must be doing the budget.

"What would you like for lunch," she asked him as she washed her hands in the sink. "Sandwiches, soup, or fried potatoes?"

"You pick," he said without looking up from his work.

"What are you working on?" she asked, as she threw a few potatoes into the sink and started peeling them.

"Just checking out our long-term accounts, savings, equity, that sort of thing."

"What for?"

"Just wondering how much we're worth. You know, if we sold everything."

"Why would we do that?"

"You never know when you might need cash more than possessions."

Emma looked at John. He had a strange, almost gloomy, look on his face. "What are you planning, John?"

He looked up. "I was just wondering. With me on the scooter half the time and you slowing down, I think it might be time for us to consider moving to Fairmount."

"The old folks' home!"

"Assisted living."

"We don't need any assistance. What do we need help with?"

John looked at her with compassion. "Cleaning, for one thing."

"I just cleaned the garage, and it looks quite nice."

"Did you mop it?"

Emma looked sheepish. "It didn't need it this time."

"And when is the last time you did mop it?" he asked, not unkindly.

Emma looked at the potatoes, still unpeeled in her hands. Then she looked at John again. "We still do our own garden. How assisted is that?"

"Didn't you tell me Frank and Edna Mae were coming over to pick and can your tomatoes?"

"They were looking for some way to help. I had to let them do something."

"And do you let Grace come and clean house for you twice a month?" Grace was John's youngest daughter.

"You know I can't get down on my knees the way I used to."

"That's just it, Emma. You can't do all that you used to do. Your kidneys are at what, half strength?"

"Dr. Teodora says that's plenty."

"And your legs, haven't they been keeping you up at nights?"

"I've been doing a lot of bending."

"No, Emma. They hurt because you're doing more than you should." He got up and came over to her side. She looked into his eyes. "You need to face it, Dear. We are both getting to the place where we need a little help. I don't want either one of us stuck, not being able to care for the other."

Tears welled up in Emma's eyes. How could she even think of leaving her home? The home she and Aaron had built so she would have a place in her old age? No! They weren't to that place yet. Nowhere near it!

John broke into her thoughts. "It's a humble person who can accept when God brings changes into their life. This is something we need to do, and we need to do it together."

Emma barely touched her lunch. Not that she tasted much of the salt-free food the doctor had restricted her to since the bladder removal, but John's announcement had swept all desires completely out of her soul. Live at Fairmount? The old folks' home?

She looked up while John was scraping his plate. "If we did go to Fairmount, could we go to one of the detached cottages? They're more like a home."

"Possibly. But the rooms in the assisted living center are not bad. I looked them over when we were there the other day.

They're nicely decorated, air-conditioned, and they don't have a kitchen. Just imagine, someone to cook for you, and you could devote your time to reading, and crocheting, and visiting. You've always loved to visit there."

"And my sewing? And gardening?"

"You could work on the quilt they keep in the room at the end of the hall. And they have that nice sitting room down by the dining room. I'm telling you, Emma, it would be as good as being in our own place, once we adjusted to the move."

"But Aaron built this place for me."

John put his hand on Emma's. "I know." He paused a moment then continued. "But if we're together, any place will feel like home."

She looked at her husband. "I have been rather tired lately."

"You've been napping more too."

"Maybe you're right," she said, as she pursed her lips and struggled to hold back her tears. "I refused you when you asked me to move to Brickerville; I won't refuse you again. Wherever you go, Mr. Horning, I shall go."

. . . .

As the day approached for them to turn in their application at the Home, Emma's right leg progressed from merely aching to being downright miserable. "Do you suppose I could use your cane today, since you'll be using the walker?" she asked John.

He looked at her with concern. "Your leg that bad?"

"It just hurts less if I baby it a bit."

"Sure. We'll pack them both along."

"You're sure you're ready to go through with the application?" he asked as they got into the car.

"I told you, wherever you go, I shall go. Besides, it's just the application. I doubt they'll have any spots available right away."

Emma was right about there not being any spots open. But within two months, Fairmount called to tell them they had a pair of adjoining rooms available in the assisted living wing. No cottages though.

"What do you think?" John asked Emma, as they sat in the Fairmount dining room enjoying a complimentary dinner of roast beef and mashed potatoes. They had received a tour of the facility and had spent a good bit of time discretely peeking into the bedrooms they passed to see how various residents had arranged their furniture.

"The rooms are nice," she admitted. "I suppose we could put both of our beds in one, and set up the other as a sort of small living room."

"They are plenty big enough," John said. "If we did that, we could have a private bathroom in our bedroom, and one the family could use when they came to visit us in the living room."

Emma laughed. "As if a private bathroom was something we need."

"You know how important the bathroom can be to old folks," John said with a wink. She gave him that phony disapproving look that let him know she got his little joke.

"I did like the view," she said. "You can see clear across the valley without getting out of your chair."

"And we'd be on the south side of the building, so you'd have sunshine all day long."

Emma thought she finally understood how the chickadees felt when she had moved their feeder. It didn't matter whether she was perched on the side of the house or under the branches of a tree—or in a pair of tiny rooms in a rest home. As long as her heavenly Father chose her dwelling place, Emma was convinced it would be the best place she could possibly be.

She looked at John. "I think we should take them. It's time."

John looked relieved.

They went home to prepare for the move. There were ninety years of accumulated possessions to sort, a freezer full of produce to distribute, a quilt to finish, and a house to sell. They finished none too soon.

Something was wrong with Emma. She could feel it in her bones. Literally. Her legs still ached, and the right one had begun to swell. And she had developed a constant, low-grade fever.

By the time they had sold their house and were fully settled in their rooms at Fairmount, she had lost her appetite.

She did the round of all the doctors, had all the normal tests. They showed nothing. But Emma knew.

"I simply don't feel as well as normal," she wrote in her diary on February 7, 2008. "I'm tired . . . wonder if this is the beginning of my end?"

Then on Tuesday, March 4, she wrote, "I don't feel well and can't eat much. I don't seem to want to recover. As thou wilt, O Lord. Strengthen me in faith."

Emma's cancer was back. Somehow, though she had surrendered her bladder and surrounding tissues to the surgeon's knife, the cancer had survived.

Had she in her stubbornness waited too long to agree to the surgery the doctors had urged her to have? Or had some unrelated cell independently changed into a cancerous state between then and now? What did it matter anyway? This cancer was not confined to a single organ as the bladder cancer had been. It was in her swollen painful leg, and in her lungs, and in her kidneys, and in her lymph nodes. There would be no stopping it this time.

"It's okay," she told John when she got the formal diagnosis. "I guess I felt it was cancer all along."

"Is that why you gave in so easily when I pressured you to move here?"

"Partly. But you didn't pressure me, John. You just talked sense into this thick, stubborn head of mine. Good thing too; I'm here where I can get cared for without having to leave you, and you're here where you can get the care you need after I'm gone."

"You know they're planning to move you down to the complete care wing? It means we won't be together."

"Sure we will. All you have to do is walk down the hall. And when you need a rest, it's a short walk back to your own bed. Besides, remember that full-time cook you were trying to sell me on? I'll be glad knowing you're eating good even when I can't cook for you."

Tears welled up in John's eyes. He squeezed Emma's hand as tightly as he dared. "I don't know if I can make it without you, Emma."

Emma returned his grip and looked at her husband, willing strength into his grieving soul.

"It's okay, John," she said. "I'm just a little bird and God is moving my feeder." She wiped the tears from her own eyes. "I understand it now. We spend our whole life thinking we are the center of the universe. And then God shifts things around and we realize it was never about us at all. It never was. It's about Him. We are just the little birds, singing the day away to make Him happy."

"I don't want you to fly away."

"We don't get to choose."

"I know," he said, the tears coursing freely down his cheeks. "I know."

. . . .

Emma's loved ones came in streams to comfort her in her last hours, Hursts and Hoovers, and Hornings. And she was one with all of them, Emma, Hurst, Hoover, Horning.

She woke one day toward the end of April to find Mark's Lucille sitting beside John.

"Am I still here?" Emma asked, surprised to find that she was still in the land of mortals.

"The Lord talked to me last night," she said, staring alternately at one then the other. "I'm so amazed that He spoke to me!"

She closed her eyes, as if concentrating, then opened them again.

"He has a record," she continued. "He wrote everything down. He told me, One more session then He'll take me home."

Emma looked at Lucille with the earnestness of one who finally understands what really matters. "I felt so little, unworthy, and a sinner."

She paused, then light, as if from the deepest core of her being, spread over her face and she smiled.

"I don't know how it's going to be, but I want to do all to be ready when He comes."

Then she closed her eyes.

A week later, Jesus visited Emma again to receive from her the only thing she had left to surrender— herself. And this time, it was forever.

I'm Free

Don't grieve for me, for now I'm free
I'm following the path God has chosen for me.
I took His hand when I heard Him call;
I turned my back and left it all.

I could not stay another day,
To laugh, to love, to work or play.
Tasks left undone must stay that way;
I've now found peace at the end of day.

If my parting has left a void,
Then fill it with remembered joys.
A friendship shared, a laugh, a kiss;
Oh yes, these things, I too will miss.
Be not burdened with times of sorrow;
Look for the sunshine of tomorrow.

My life's been full, I savored much;
Good friends, good times, a loved one's touch.
Perhaps my time seems all too brief;
Don't lengthen your pain with undue grief.
Lift up your heart and peace to thee,
God wanted me now—He set me free.

AUTHOR: SHANNON LEE MOSELEY

Historical note: Emma died on the evening of April 29, 2007
in her room at Fairmount Home.

Sources

CHAPTER 1

Burkholder, Edith. Unpublished article on Emma's life (circa. 1975), 1-3 and attached sheet.

Hoover, Lamar. Letter to the author, October, 27, 2012.

Hurst and Hoover families. Interviews, October 2012.

Hurst, Emma. Journals, no. 1 (1992), 3-19.

Hurst, Emma. Journals, no. 2 (1978-1987), January, 27, 1980.

Hurst, Emma. Letter to niece Marie, April, 3, 2003.

Hurst, Emma. Life Story, unpublished, October 31, 2006.

Hurst, Emma. Memories (2007), February 8, April 18-20, July 17-18.

Hurst, Esther. "Memories of Her Early Years," undated.

Hurst, Lydia. "Memories of Her Early Years," undated.

Zimmerman, Jolene and Regina. emails with author, 2012-2013.

CHAPTER 2

Burkholder, Edith. Unpublished article on Emma's life (circa. 1975), 3-6.

Hurst and Hoover families. Interviews, October 2012.

Hurst, Alta. "Memories of Her Early Years," undated.

Hurst, Emma. Journals, no. 1 (1992), 13-18.

Hurst, Emma. Journals, no. 2 (1978-1987), January, 27, 1980.

Hurst, Emma. Life Story, unpublished, October 31, 2006.

Hurst, Emma. Memories (2007), August 22.

Hurst, Esther. "Memories of Her Early Years," undated.

Hurst et. al. Descendants of Frank W. Hurst 1863-2000.
Morgantown, PA: Masthof Press, 2002.

Hurst, Lydia. "Memories of Her Early Years," October, 27, 2012.

Hurst, Lydia. Memories of My Mother, July 25, 1992.

Hurst, Paul. "Memories of His Early Years," November, 1996.

Hurst, Paul. Photograph of the Hurst Farm circa. 1968 in A Pleasant View
of Martindale, Earl Township, Lancaster County, PA, 1733-1933.
No publisher or publication date.

Zimmerman, Jolene and Regina. emails with author, (2012-2013).

CHAPTER 3

Burkholder, Edith. Unpublished article on Emma's life (circa. 1975), 3, 6-8.

Hurst and Hoover families. Interviews, October 2012.

Hurst, Emma. Journals, no. 1 (1992), 20-27.

Hurst, Emma. Journals, no. 2 (1978-1987), January, 27, 1980.

Hurst, Emma. Life Story, unpublished, October 31, 2006.

Hurst, Emma. Memories (2007), November 2-4.

Hurst, Esther. "Memories of Her Early Years," undated.

Hurst et. al. Descendants of Frank W. Hurst 1863-2000. Morgantown, PA:
Masthof Press, 2002.

Hurst, Katie. Diary (1941-1942).

Hurst, Lydia. Letter to the author, October 27, 2012.

Hurst, Lydia. "Memories of Her Early Years," undated.

Hurst, Paul. "Memories of His Early Years," November, 1996.

Zimmerman, Jolene and Regina. emails with author, (2012-2013).

CHAPTER 4

Burkholder, Edith. Unpublished article on Emma's life (circa. 1975), 6-8.

Hurst and Hoover families. Interviews, October 2012.

Hurst, Emma. Journals, no. 1 (1992), 25-27.

Hurst, Emma. Journals, no. 2 (1978-1987), January, 27, 1980.

Hurst, Emma. Life Story, unpublished, October 31, 2006.

Hurst et. al. Descendants of Frank W. Hurst 1863-2000. Morgantown, PA: Masthof Press, 2002.

Hurst, Katie. Diary (1941-1942).

Hurst, Paul. "Memories of His Early Years," November, 1996.

Matthews, Mark. Smoke Jumping on the Western Fire Line: Conscientious Objectors During World War II. University of Oklahoma Press, Norman, 2006.

Tobacco Lore of Lancaster County, Pennsylvania at, http://www.horse-shoe.cc/pennadutch/people/trades/tobacco/ tobacco.xhtm, Retrieved November 2012

Smith, Hannah Whitall. A Christian's Secret of a Happy Life, Revell. 1988.

Zimmerman, Jolene and Regina. emails with author, (2012-2013).

CHAPTER 5

Burkholder, Edith. Unpublished article on Emma's life (circa. 1975), 9-11.

Court Records for Docket no. 66, Emma, B. Hurst, for September, 1946 session of Lancaster County Criminal Court, on microfiche at Lancaster Clerk of Courts, Criminal.

Hurst and Hoover families. Interviews, October 2012.

Hurst, Emma. Journals, no. 2 (1978-1987), January, 27, 1980.

Hurst, Emma. Journals, no. 3 (1988-2007), April 10, 1991.

Hurst, Emma. Life Story, unpublished, October 31, 2006.

Hurst, Emma. Loose journal sheets, (1937-1947).

Hurst, Emma. Memories (2007), August 30.

Intelligencer Journal, September, 11, 1946, January 11, 1947.

Lancaster New Era, September, 10 1946, September 11, 1946, January 10, 1947.

Sunrise and Sunset Calculator, www.sunrisesunset.com/calendar.asp. Retrieved November 1, 2012.

Trolley Cars on Duke Street at Orange Street, circa. 1940, photographic print no. 2-04-06-0, Lancaster Historical Society.

Where Fredrick crosses N. Duke Street, Lancaster, Pa, sometime post 1907, postcard no. 911-005-003, Lancaster Historical Society. www.lancasterhistory.org. Retrieved October 25, 2012.

Zimmerman, Jolene. The Life of Emma, 2007, 1-2.

Zimmerman, Jolene and Regina. emails with author (2012-2013).

CHAPTER 6

Burkholder, Edith. Unpublished article on Emma's life (circa. 1975), 11-14.

Court Records for Docket no. 66, Emma B. Hurst, for September, 1946 session of Lancaster County Criminal Court, on microfiche at Lancaster Clerk of Courts, Criminal.

Hurst and Hoover families. Interviews, October 2012.

Hurst, Emma. Journals, no. 2 (1978-1987), January, 27, 1980.

Hurst, Emma. Journals, no. 3 (1988-2007), April 10, 1991.

Hurst, Emma. Life Story, unpublished, October 31, 2006.

Hurst, Emma. Loose journal sheets, (1937-1947).

Intelligencer Journal, September, 11, 1946, January 11, 1947.

Lancaster New Era, September, 10 1946, September 11, 1946, January 10, 1947. www.lancasterhistory.org. Retrieved October 25, 2012.

Zimmerman, Jolene and Regina. emails with author (2012-2013).

CHAPTER 7

Burkholder, Edith. Unpublished article on Emma's life (circa. 1975),14-17.

Court Records for Docket no. 66, Emma B. Hurst, for September, 1946 session of Lancaster County Criminal Court, on microfiche at Lancaster Clerk of Courts, Criminal.

Court Records for Dockets no. 192 and 193, Bertha and Vergie Flowers, for June, 1946 session of Lancaster County Criminal Court, on microfiche at Lancaster Clerk of Courts, Criminal.

Flowers, Bertha. Letter to Emma's step-mother, undated.

Hurst and Hoover families. Interviews, October 2012.

Hurst, Emma. Journals, no. 2 (1978-1987), January, 27, 1980.

Hurst, Emma. Journals, no. 3 (1988-2007), April 10, 1991.

Hurst, Emma. Letter to an unnamed cousin, February 23, 1947.

Hurst, Emma. Letter to her family, January 12, 1947.

Hurst, Emma. Letter to her family, April 6, 1947.

Hurst, Emma. Letter to Verna Hoover, March 21, 1947.

Hurst, Emma. Life Story, unpublished, October 31, 2006.

Hurst, Emma. Loose journal sheets (1937-1947).

Hurst, Emma. Memories (2007), July 8.

Hurst, Emma. "Sketch of My Jail Cell," 1947.

www.lancasterhistory.org. Retrieved October 12, 2012.

Zimmerman, Jolene and Regina. emails with author, (2012-2013).

CHAPTER 8

Horning, Moses M. A Chair Shop of My Own, loose article with no date or magazine name.

Hurst and Hoover families. Interviews, October 2012.

Hurst, Emma. Diaries (1948).

Hurst, Emma. Journals, no. 1 (1992), 28-29.

Hurst, Emma. Journals, no. 2 (1978-1987), January, 27, 1980.

Hurst, Emma. Life Story, unpublished, October 31, 2006.

Hurst, Emma. Loose journal sheets (1947-1957).

Hurst, Emma. Memories (2007), February 11, June 9.

CHAPTER 9

Hurst and Hoover families. Interviews, October 2012.

Hurst, Emma. Diaries (1948).

Hurst, Emma. Journals, no. 1 (1992), 29-31.

Hurst, Emma. Journals, no. 2 (1978-1987), January, 27, 1980.

Hurst, Emma. Life Story, unpublished, October 31, 2006.

Hurst, Emma. Loose journal sheets, (1947-1957).

Hurst, Paul. Telephone interview, December 31, 2012.

The Laurel Wreath, Yearbook of Lancaster Mennonite School, 1954.

CHAPTER 10

http://www.christian-history.org/felix-manz-martyrdom.html Retrieved. 1/28/13.

http://www.reformationhappens.com/people/manz. Retrieved 1/28/13.

Hurst and Hoover families. Interviews, October 2012.

Hurst, Emma, compiler. A Day by Day Diary of Europe and The Holy Land Tour. Kalona, Iowa: Enos & Ada Miller, 1956.

Hurst, Emma. Journals, no. 1 (1992), 31-32.

Hurst, Emma. Life Story, unpublished, October 31, 2006.

Hurst, Emma. Memories (2007), February 20, February 28, November 4.

Lancaster New Era, October 13, 1955.

Van Braght, Thieleman J., The Martyrs Mirror. Scottdale &Waterloo: Herald Press, 1950.

CHAPTER 11

Burkholder, Edith. Unpublished article on Emma's life (circa. 1975), 18-20.

The EMC Weather Vane, September 27, 1957, October 25, 1957, November 8, 1957, March 21, 1957.

Hurst and Hoover families. Interviews, October 2012.

Hurst, Emma. Journals, no. 1 (1992), 32-35.

Hurst, Emma. Journals, no. 2 (1978-1987), January, 27, 1980, November 9, 1987.

Hurst, Emma. Life Story, unpublished, October 31, 2006.

Hurst, Emma. Memories, (2007) April 20, June 30.

Pellman, Hubert R., Eastern Mennonite College, 1917-1967 - A History. Eastern Mennonite College Press (1967), 180-199.

Shenandoah, Yearbook of Eastern Mennonite College, 1961.

Smith, Hannah Whitall. A Christian's Secret of a Happy Life, Revell, 1988.

CHAPTER 12

Burkholder, Edith. Unpublished article on Emma's life (circa. 1975),18-20.

Hurst and Hoover families. Interviews, October 2012.

Hurst, Emma. Journals, no. 1 (1992), 35-37.

Hurst, Emma. Journals, no. 2 (1978-1987).

Hurst, Emma. Life Story, unpublished, October 31, 2006.

Nolt, James K. Emma H. Horning's School Teaching Experiences: Reflections and Interview. April, 2005.

Open House, pamphlet for Blueball School and Union Grove School, May 19, 1962.

Zimmerman, H. Daniel. A Blessing to Many (2010), 7-10.

CHAPTER 13

Burkholder, Edith. Unpublished article on Emma's life (circa. 1975), 20.

Hurst and Hoover families. Interviews, October 2012.

Hurst, Emma. Journals, no. 2 (1978-1987).

Hurst, Emma. Journals, no. 3 (1987-2004), April 6, 1996.

Hurst, Emma. Life Story, unpublished, October 31, 2006.

Hurst, Emma. Memories (2007), April 9, May 29, December 7.

Sensenig, Donna. email, November 3, 2012.

Zimmerman, Jolene. email to the author, April 5, 2013.

CHAPTER 14

Burkholder, Edith. Unpublished article on Emma's life (circa. 1975), 20.

Hurst and Hoover families. Interviews, October 2012.

Hurst, Emma. Journals, no. 2 (1978-1987).

Hurst, Emma. Memories (2007), February 19, June 1.

Weaver, Mary Hoover. Selected journal entries from 1968-1973 as compiled by daughter Ruth Horning.

http://www.allabouthistory.org/school-prayer.html, Retrieved 3/28/13.

Zimmerman, Jolene. email to the author, April 5, 2013.

CHAPTER 15

Burkholder, Edith. Unpublished article on Emma's life (circa. 1975), 20-24.

Horning, Ruth. email, November, 2012.

Horst, Beatrice. From old typewritten sheets by Beatrice undated and emailed to the author by Jolene Zimmerman on April 4, 2013.

Hurst and Hoover families. Interviews, October 2012.

Hurst, Emma. Journals, no. 2 (1978-1987).

Hurst, Emma. Life Story. unpublished, October 31, 2006.

Hurst, Emma. Memories (2007), February 19, June 1.

Hurst, Emma. Our Accident, unpublished, July 28, 1973.

The Penny Saver, August 8, 1973.

Zimmerman, Jolene. email to the author, April 5, 2013.

CHAPTER 16

Burkholder, Edith. Letter to the family, May 17, 2008.

Burkholder, Edith. Letter to the author, December, 2012.

Burkholder, Edith. Unpublished article on Emma's life (circa. 1975), 24-31.

Hurst and Hoover families. Interviews, October 2012.

Hurst, Emma. Diaries (1975).

Hurst, Emma. Journals, no. 2 (1978-1987).

Hurst, Emma. Memories (2007), February 19, June 1.

Snyder, Rhoda. Letter to author, November 4, 2012.

Zimmerman, Jolene. email to the author, April 5, 2013.

Zimmerman, Jolene. email to the author on November 4, 2012.

CHAPTER 17

Burkholder, Edith. Letter to the family, May 17, 2008.

Burkholder, Edith. Letter to the author, December, 2012.

Burkholder, Edith. Unpublished article on Emma's life (circa. 1975), 24-31.

Hurst and Hoover families. Interviews, October 2012.

Hurst, Emma. Journals, no. 2 (1978-1987).

Hurst, Emma. Life Story, unpublished, October 31, 2006.

Hurst, Emma. Memories (2007), April 3.

Hurst, Emma. Our Accident, unpublished, July 28, 1973.

Zimmerman, Jolene. email to the author, April 5, 2013.

CHAPTER 18

Burkholder, Edith. Unpublished article on Emma's life (circa. 1975), 27-31.

Horning, Ruth Ann. Letter to author, 2013.

Hurst and Hoover families. Interviews, October 2012.

Hurst, Emma. Diaries, (1975).

Hurst, Emma. Journals, no. 2 (1978-1987).

Hurst, Emma. Life Story, unpublished, October 31, 2006.

Sensenig, Donna. email, November 3, 2012.

Weaver, Mary Hoover. Selected Journal from 1973 as compiled by daughter Ruth.

Zimmerman, Jolene. email to the author, April 5, 2013.

CHAPTER 19

Hurst and Hoover families. Interviews, October 2012.

Hurst, Emma. Diaries, (1975).

Hurst, Emma. Journals, no. 2 (1978-1987).

Hurst, Emma. Journals, no. 3 (1987-2004).

Hurst, Emma. Memories (2007), October 19.

Zimmerman, Jolene. email to the author, April 5, 2013.

CHAPTER 20

Burkholder, Edith. Letter to the author, December, 2012.

Hurst and Hoover families. Interviews, October 2012.

Hurst, Emma. Diaries, (1992).

Hurst, Emma. Journals, no. 2 (1978-1987).

Hurst, Emma. Journals, no. 3 (1987-2004).

Hurst, Emma. Life Story, unpublished, October 31, 2006.

Hurst, Emma. Memories (2007), Aug 15.

Nolt, James K. email to the author, February 2, 2013.

Nolt, James K. Emma H. Horning's School Teaching Experiences: Reflections and Interview. April, 2005.

Sensenig, Donna. email, November 3, 2012.

Zimmerman, Jolene. email to the author, April 5, 2013.

CHAPTER 21

Hurst and Hoover families. Interviews, October 2012.

Hurst, Emma. Diaries (1992).

Hurst, Emma. Diaries, (1993), unnumbered.

Hurst, Emma. Journals, no. 3 (1987-2004).

Hurst, Emma. Life Story, unpublished, October 31, 2006.

Zimmerman, Regina. emails to author. August 16, and September 6, 2012.

CHAPTER 22

Hurst and Hoover families. Interviews, October 2012.

Hurst, Emma. Diaries (1993).

Hurst, Emma. Journals, no. 3 (1987-2004).

Hurst, Emma. Life Story, unpublished, October 31, 2006.

Martin, John and Esther. Letter to author, undated.

CHAPTER 23

Burkholder, Edith. Letter to author, December 2012.

Hurst and Hoover families. Interviews, October 2012.

Hurst, Emma. Diaries (1993).

Hurst, Emma. Diaries (1994-95).

Hurst, Emma. Diaries (1996-April 1999).

Hurst, Emma. Diaries (April 1999-2000).

Hurst, Emma. Journals, no. 3 (1987-2004).

Hurst, Emma. Life Story, unpublished, October 31, 2000.

Hurst, Emma. Memories (2007), October 19, November 5.

CHAPTER 24

Hurst and Hoover families. Interviews, October 2012.

Hurst, Emma. Journals, no. 3 (1987-2004).

Hurst, Emma. Diaries (April 1999-2000).

Hurst, Emma. Diaries (2004-November 26, 2005).

Hurst, Emma. Memories (2007), July 22, October 19, October 27.

Snyder, Rhoda. Letter to the author, October 27, 2012.

CHAPTER 25

Hurst and Hoover families. Interviews, October 2012.

Hurst, Emma. Diaries (2004-November 26, 2005).

Hurst, Emma. Journals, no. 3 (1987-2004).

Hurst, Emma. Memories (2007), August 28.

Zimmerman, Regina. email to author, November 6, 2012.

CHAPTER 26

Hurst and Hoover families. Interviews, October 2012.

Hurst, Emma. Diaries (2004-November 26, 2005).

Hurst, Emma. Diaries (2006-2007).

CHAPTER 27

Burkholder, Edith. Unpublished article on Emma's life (circa. 1975), 1-3 and attached sheet. May 17, 2008.

Horning, Lucille. Account of a visit she had with Emma a week before her death.

Horning, Sylvia. email to the author on June 28, 2013.

Hurst and Hoover families. Interviews, October 2012.

Hurst, Emma. Diaries (2006-2007).

Hurst, Emma. Diaries (January 1-March 23, 2008).

Hurst, Emma. Letter to family, March 27, 2008.

Zimmerman, Jolene. email to the author on 11/4/12.

Adopted

MCGURRIN . $9.99

250 PAGES . PAPERBACK . ITEM# ADO37251

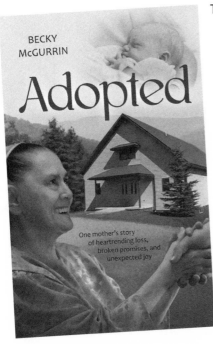

This is the day you give up the most precious thing you've ever been given, Pat said in a quiet, sad corner of her mind. The time had come, the last time she would see her daughter—forever. Pat's decision to place Suzanne for adoption haunted her for years. The true story of a woman whose life of disappointment and loss was transformed by her growing awareness of a God who surprised and blessed her beyond what she ever imagined.

one mother's story

OF HEARTRENDING LOSS, BROKEN PROMISES, AND UNEXPECTED JOY

Order Form

To order, send this completed order form to:

Vision Publishers
P.O. Box 190
Harrisonburg, VA 22803
Fax: 540-437-1969
E-mail: orders@vision-publishers.com
www.vision-publishers.com

_____   _____
Name   Date

_____   _____
Mailing Address   Phone

_____
City   State   Zip

From Streetlights to Stars Qty. _____ x $9.99 ea. = _____

Adopted Qty. _____ x $9.99 ea. = _____

(Please call for quantity discounts - 877-488-0901)

Price _____

Virginia residents add 5% sales tax _____

Ohio residents add applicable sales tax _____

Shipping & handling **$4.20**

❑ Check #_____   Grand Total _____

❑ Money Order   ❑ Visa

❑ MasterCard   ❑ Discover   **All Payments in US Dollars**

Name on Card _____

Card #__|__|__|__| __|__|__|__| __|__|__|__| __|__|__|__|

3-digit code from signature panel __|__|__| Exp. Date __|__|__|__|

Thank you for your order!

For a complete listing of our books request our catalog.
Bookstore inquiries welcome

Order Form

To order, send this completed order form to:

Vision Publishers
P.O. Box 190
Harrisonburg, VA 22803
Fax: 540-437-1969
E-mail: orders@vision-publishers.com
www.vision-publishers.com

_____   _____
Name   Date

_____   _____
Mailing Address   Phone

_____
City   State   Zip

From Streetlights to Stars Qty. _____ x $9.99 ea. = _____

Adopted Qty. _____ x $9.99 ea. = _____

(Please call for quantity discounts - 877-488-0901)

Price _____

Virginia residents add 5% sales tax _____

Ohio residents add applicable sales tax _____

Shipping & handling __**$4.20**__

❑ Check #_____   Grand Total _____

❑ Money Order   ❑ Visa

❑ MasterCard   ❑ Discover   **All Payments in US Dollars**

Name on Card _____

Card #__|__|__|__| __|__|__|__| __|__|__|__| __|__|__|__|

3-digit code from signature panel__|__|__| Exp. Date __|__|__|__|

Thank you for your order!

For a complete listing of our books request our catalog.
Bookstore inquiries welcome